This Advance Reader's Edition is an uncorrected version of the book. All quotations from the text should be checked for accuracy either against a finished copy of the book or, if not available, with the Palgrave Macmillan Publicity Department.

The Face *of* Emotion

THE
FACE *of*
EMOTION

How Botox Affects Our
Mood and Relationships

Eric Finzi, MD

palgrave
macmillan

THE FACE OF EMOTION
Copyright © Eric Finzi, MD, 2013.

All rights reserved.

First published in 2013 by PALGRAVE MACMILLAN*—a division of St. Martin's Press LLC, 175 Fifth Avenue, New York, NY 10010.

Where this book is distributed in the UK, Europe and the rest of the world, this is by Palgrave Macmillan, a division of Macmillan Publishers Limited, registered in England, company number 785998, of Houndmills, Basingstoke, Hampshire RG21 6XS.

Palgrave Macmillan is the global academic imprint of the above companies and has companies and representatives throughout the world.

Palgrave* and Macmillan* are registered trademarks in the United States, the United Kingdom, Europe and other countries.

ISBN 978–0–230–34185–2

Library of Congress Cataloging-in-Publication Data is available from the Library of Congress.

A catalogue record of the book is available from the British Library.

Design by Newgen Imaging Systems, Ltd., Chennai, India

First edition: January 2013

10 9 8 7 6 5 4 3 2 1

Printed in the United States of America.

CONTENTS

ACKNOWLEDGMENTS

THIS BOOK WAS born when Jay Leno made some rather amusing jokes based on my research on Botox. My agent-to-be, Kathleen Anderson, astutely realized that I had touched a societal nerve: her persuasiveness convinced me to assemble the pieces of the puzzle. Thank you, Kathy, for giving a guiding hand throughout the entire process.

My wife Lalage piqued my curiosity about facial expressions when she started discussing the work of the British neurologist Jonathan Cole. She, my daughter Dawn, and my son Marc have endured many discussions about the face. Special thanks to Scott Norton, who stimulated my thinking about Botox. I am indebted to the many researchers who performed all the psychological investigations that triggered my interest in the field: Paul Ekman, Robert Provine, Richard Davidson, Joseph LeDoux, Antonio Damasio, Robert Zajonc, Gary Schwartz, Martin Seligman, Fritz Strack, and Paula Niedenthal.

I dedicate this book to my mother Hilda, who nurtured my artistic side from my earliest years. Ultimately, it was through painting that I began my research about the face.

I am indebted to my patients, who have freely told their stories to me and made me realize how much was right in front of me, if only I opened my eyes. Special thanks to my sister Rima Finzi-Strauss, who helped critique many parts of this book. Mark Eisner helped interview patients and assisted in early research. Nathalie Jules helped with figures. Michelle Delino helped me navigate the world of media. Hilary Hinzmann provided valuable criticism, suggestions, and editorial help in the early stages of the book. He was a pleasure to work with. Ann Patty provided excellent editorial advice. Donna Cherry and Laura Lancaster at Palgrave Macmillan were very helpful. Natalie Turner helped get permission for the photographs. Special thanks to my editor at Palgrave Macmillan, Luba Ostashevsky, who really had a vision for what needed to be in this book. Her dedication and insight improved this book.

INTRODUCTION

I DIDN'T UNDERSTAND what I saw, but I knew it was important. They didn't teach psychology in third grade, but I was hardwired to react to what my mother was expressing in her face. She was sitting up in bed—an unusual place for her since she almost always managed to get up and moving, no matter how she felt on the inside. But this day was different. Mom looked at me with a deeply etched and furrowed brow. In retrospect, her face was etched from many moments of angst, moments hidden except by the telltale signs between her eyes. That day her frown spoke to me in a very visceral way, alerting me to her inner suffering, removing me from my normal oblivious self.

When I was a kid, my thoughts usually centered around my next game of catch with my best friend George, who lived a few doors down. But for some reason I still remember that day today. I was used to hearing my mother complain about her physical health (her mental suffering often transmuted to a litany of physical complaints) and was usually able to store her words in a quiet part of my brain. But my mind would not let me ignore her palpable frown, which made an indelible impression on my unconscious.

We now know that facial expressions are innate, expressed by babies and the blind, evolutionarily conserved in humans across cultures and in our closest primate relatives, fundamentally understood as well by preliterate humans as by college students. And as we shall discover, anything so conserved by nature over generations is crucial to our health and well-being. The face has a privileged role in our lives, for our emotions, feelings, and relationships. My brain was programmed to pay attention to and give me continuous updates of a fellow human's facial expression and to get upset by a powerful frown.

Mom was depressed, and her facial muscles were talking. I heard her clearly, even if I did not yet have the words to help conceptualize the feelings that her pained brow imparted to me. Fortunately, you don't need formal schooling to be able to empathize with the expression of sadness on your mother's face. Here again your face has an active role, as your unconscious mimicking of another's facial expression helps you to understand what they are feeling, what they are experiencing.

Years later I would ask myself what my mother's frown really meant and how it was connected to her inner pain. Why did I remember it so vividly? How could a facial expression disturb me so?

Through a convergence of unlikely events, I began to discover the answers to these questions as I came to realize how important our faces are for causing as well as expressing emotions. I was empowered by being a physician working outside his specialty, less inhibited by not being a mental health professional, less aware of what was accepted to "be right," less worried about upsetting the applecart. If you are an outsider, you have less to lose by coming up with an idea that was made into a joke on a Jay Leno show (true).

Generally, we assume that our facial expressions reflect rather than direct our emotions of the moment. Yet much evidence suggests that our facial expressions are not secondary to, but rather a central driving force of, our emotions. Our emotions are embodied by our faces, embodied by the muscles that help move our lips, our eyes, our eyebrows. Feelings are not just abstract constructs floating around in an ether called our minds. Rather, our brains use all the literal tools accumulated over millions of years of evolution. If you smile broadly, at that moment you *will* feel happier. You need your smile to help you "feel" the emotion. Conversely, frowning will negatively affect your thinking, coloring your view of the world around you. This simple fact could positively influence the health of many, but it has not yet entered contemporary thought as a useful part of our understanding of emotions and moods.

This book tries to explain the powerful connections between our smiles and frowns and our emotions, feelings, moods, and mental health. My belief in the power of art to enrich our understanding of ourselves led me to weave artistic as well as scientific threads into the fabric of these pages. It was through art that I initially wandered into the field of facial expressions, and the insights of artists sometimes prefigure by centuries what scientists ultimately show.

I have been a dermatologic surgeon for twenty years, and I regularly witness how changing a person's face not only affects her relationships with others but also with herself. This idea is so counterintuitive that it bears repeating: the facial expression you make can affect how *you* feel, independent of any social interactions.

Botox has long been a part of my cosmetic tools, softening lines and turning back the clock. But it took me a while to realize its potential to do so much more. It is a very selective inhibitor of muscles, allowing one to pinpoint which muscles to treat. As I became aware of an important feedback loop between the brain and the muscles of facial expression, I began to suspect that Botox could help control the flow of negative emotions, quieting the facial muscles that really express negativity, the muscles between the eyebrows that help create the frown. Could I change moods and help depression simply by preventing a negative facial expression?

In 2003 I began a clinical trial to test my hypothesis that Botox inhibition of the frown muscle could help depressed patients. Working with a clinical psychologist, Erika Wasserman, I placed Botox into ten patients' frown muscles, right between the eyebrows.

In order to be eligible for the study, patients were evaluated for depressive symptomatology and needed to meet the American Psychiatric Association's *Diagnostic and Statistical Manual of Mental Disorders* (*DSM–IV*) criteria for major depression. In addition, only patients with a Beck Depression Inventory (BDI) II score of 20 or greater showing moderate to severe depression were eligible. The BDI has become one of the most widely accepted instruments for detecting depression and assessing its severity. Each patient needed to have at least a six-month history of depression. Most of the patients in my study had been depressed for years.

Two months after the Botox injection, the majority of patients in the initial trial were no longer clinically depressed by *DSM–IV* criteria or by their BDI–II test scores. Everyone always assumes that people felt better because they looked better—but then why don't we just prescribe plastic surgery for depressed patients? Because it doesn't work.

Some of the patients in the study didn't have any visible frown lines before the injections, suggesting that they didn't feel better just because they looked better, since there was *no* cosmetic improvement. I'm not disputing that looking good makes you feel good, but you can look wonderful on the outside and still feel terrible psychic pain on the inside. Beautiful people suffer from serious depression. Beauty was no protection for Brooke Shields when she developed her postpartum depression. Think of Ophelia, that ethereal beauty whose tragic fate was so often depicted by the pre-Raphaelite painters. The contrast between her sadness and her beauty is part of the allure of this Shakespearean tale.

Our journey here reveals the many-splendored roles of facial expressions: how they help navigate our social interactions with our fellow humans, how they help us make decisions, how they help us feel our own emotions and those of others, and how they do it all largely hidden from our conscious view. To make these discoveries, I needed to explore not just the experiments, but also my subjects' lives, in part like a natural historian, anthropologist, psychologist, artist, surgeon—but most of all like a physician scientist who was called on to remain open to uncovering the surprises about our expressions that operate so seamlessly, and are so commonplace, that they are really hard to see. The narratives I relate are about my patients, my family, and acquaintances who have been kind enough to help me understand their stories and, in the process, help me understand more about what it is to be human.

CHAPTER 1

A POISON TO SOME

A MIRACLE TO OTHERS

"What is now proved was once only imagined."

—William Blake

WE ARE BOMBARDED on a daily basis with flawless images of women and men. Whether real or enhanced digitally and/or surgically, these young movie stars and models become idols whose looks and actions are emulated by millions. From style to parenting to cosmetic procedures, these demigods provide an elusive standard to which many aspire.

The desire to look like these icons goes hand in hand with the wish to prevent or reverse the ravages of aging, a part of human behavior for as long as we have had records. For millennia we have searched for simple, quick, and effective ways of treating aging. Today, Botox has become the most popular cosmetic procedure in the world. What attributes of Botox account for its immense popularity?

Perhaps it is because Botox injections are quick, affordable (as cosmetic procedures go), almost painless, and effective at reducing lines and wrinkles. In addition, treatment with Botox is non-invasive, is safe, causes minimal bruising, and requires only a short recovery period. All of these features add up to a drug used by millions.

How surprising then is the vitriolic reaction that the discussion of Botox can elicit! What is it about this molecule that brings out big partisan guns at the dinner table? How many other small proteins have such strong emotions attached to them?

What Is Botox?

Botox is a trademarked name for one type of chemical whose scientific name is botulinum toxin A. It is derived from a bacterium that lives best under conditions where there is no oxygen. Before there were safety standards for the canning of food, it was not rare for people to die from the ingestion of this bacteria and its toxin after eating a can of improperly prepared food. Botulinum toxin is the most powerful poison made by nature. A single gram of the purified toxin, widely dispersed and inhaled, could kill a million people.

How Botox Was Discovered

In 1822, Justinus Kerner published his insights on the clinical course of botulism, including physical findings such as lack of tear fluid and muscle paralysis. Amazingly enough, he also speculated on the potential therapeutic value of botulinum toxin, including its possible use to prevent abnormal muscle movements. Subsequently, the bacterium responsible for botulism was identified and cultured. Long before any of the current uses, research was focused on purifying the toxin for use in warfare. Fortunately, botulinum toxin did not prove to be an easily applied weapon; it was more suited as a medicine. It wasn't until 1973, when Dr. Alan Scott first published his work on the treatment of strabismus (a disorder in which the eyes are not properly aligned with one another, usually resulting from a lack of coordination from muscles controlling eye movements) in monkeys with botulinum toxin, that the possibilities for botulinum toxin being used medically began to be explored.

Botulinum toxin cosmetic uses were discovered when Jean Carruthers, a Canadian ophthalmologist, was treating a patient in 1987 for a rare eye disorder known as blepharospasm that causes excessive blinking of the eyes and, in some, causes the eyelids to slam shut. Dr. Carruthers treated the woman with botulinum toxin, a then largely unknown substance. Application of botulinum toxin in small amounts worked well and stopped Dr. Carruthers's patient's debilitating eye disorder. But, even with no symptoms, the patient kept coming back, telling her doctor that each time she received a botulinum toxin injection, the wrinkles between her brows seemed to disappear, giving her a relaxed, untroubled expression.

Jean's husband, Alastair, a dermatologist, found the story of the blepharospasm patient intriguing and began to explore how botulinum toxin could be used to enhance a person's appearance. Alastair and Jean's seminal research helped bring botulinum toxin into wide usage. Since then, millions have been treated with botulinum toxin for both cosmetic and non-cosmetic reasons.

The toxin prevents neurons from releasing the chemical that allows us to use our muscles. A tiny amount prevents muscles from performing their normal duties, such as swallowing and breathing. If you ingest enough of the toxin, it paralyzes all the muscles in your body, including the ones necessary for moving the diaphragm, which is a required part of breathing. Unless you are hooked up to a breathing machine, you do not survive long after ingesting that bad can of food. In the 1800s, eating a contaminated sausage would cause a slow and agonizing death as one's whole body became progressively weaker until, finally, one was unable to breathe. But injected locally, in tiny doses, the toxin paralyzes only a small area of muscle. The effect is temporary, lasting 3 to 12 months depending on where it is injected. In the face it is usually injected into the upper third to diminish forehead lines, crow's feet, and frowning between the eyebrows. Any lines on the face that are caused by underlying facial muscle movement are helped by Botox. The ability to smile with your mouth is not affected, and you look younger from the softening of lines and creases and the absence of a scowl between your eyebrows.

It sounds pretty nasty that you are injecting a poison—until you realize that almost all drugs, in the wrong dose, are poisons. What really matters is the difference between the effective and lethal doses of the drug. The bigger the difference, the safer the drug. Conversely, if there is not much distinction between the dangerous and the effective dose, one must be very careful. Let us take the example of the drug acetaminophen, known most commonly by its brand name Tylenol. It is a safe drug when used properly, as evidenced by the millions of children who take it every year (who would give a poison to their child?). But what happens if you ingest ten times as many Tylenol as recommended? This is one of the more common reasons that young people require liver transplantation.

Or how about trying to push away some anxiety with a few Valium and a couple of drinks to further numb the pain? Another very bad idea. This sort of combination has accidently killed quite a few in Hollywood because the ratio between the lethal dose and the effective dose of anti-anxiety pills is not very high to begin with and is lowered significantly when combined with alcohol. Quite a few drugs have dangerous interactions with other medicines that can alter their safety profile. Botox is not among them. The difference between effective and lethal doses of botulinum toxin is huge.

If someone accidentally injected 20 times as much botulinum toxin as needed into your face, it would not kill you (although your face would look frozen). The fact that botulinum toxin is such a powerful and specific poison actually makes it a relatively safer drug. If you take 20 times the proper dose of aspirin, the pain in your shoulder may go away only to be replaced by more severe stomach pain caused by a bleeding ulcer, one of the unfortunate side effects of aspirin. In order for aspirin to help your shoulder, it needs to enter your bloodstream. But for it to get there, you need to eat it. And 20 pills can make quite a hole in your stomach.

Even normal doses of certain drugs can occasionally have unpleasant side effects. Take the popular drug Bactrim, which is commonly used to treat urinary tract infections. Occasionally it causes a serious reaction called Stevens-Johnson syndrome. The rash can be life threatening and may appear after one normal dose.

Many of my skin cancer patients are older and are taking blood thinners for their cardiovascular disease. One of the most common is Coumadin (Warfarin). This drug does a beautiful job of inhibiting your ability to form a clot, which is helpful when trying to prevent heart attacks or strokes. But Warfarin is a tricky molecule. If you take three times as much as you need for your heart, you might bleed to death. It is also, for the same reason, one of the most effective poisons for rats. But I don't think that most of my patients know that every day they are swallowing a rat poison. If they did, they would probably be put off by it. One can just imagine how well the pills would sell if the bottle had a boxed warning about the danger of feeding the pills to rats. Warfarin is such a useful drug because it is such a good poison.

Botulinum toxin does indeed derive from a poison. But then so do many of our great drugs. Penicillin, the magical wonder drug that helped introduce the antibiotic revolution to modern medicine, is actually a poison made by a certain fungus that wished to kill the bacteria around it. The fungus makes it to "poison" its enemy, the bacteria. No one would deny the life-saving features of antibiotics. But I have had patients who were perfectly rational in every other facet of their care, who, when I bring up the possibility of using Botox, said, "Oh no, I could never use that." They have heard that it is a toxin, a poison. They wanted other alternatives to soften a crease or a furrow.

Some of our best blood pressure medicines are derived from plant poisons that Stone Age tribes of humans living in tropical rain forests discovered to be powerful when placed at the end of their blow darts. When their prey or tribal enemy was hit by a poison dart, their blood pressure lowered enough that they collapsed and died. Their poison darts led to the discovery of a whole class of medicines that lower blood pressure. But personal risk assessment, unless you are a statistician, usually does not reflect reality. How otherwise to explain why many prefer to drive rather than fly 900 miles because it feels safer?

In contrast with most other drugs, botulinum toxin in normal doses stays where it is put: an injection into the forehead will have no effect anywhere else in your body. The fear that botulinum toxin generates because of its poisonous origins is understandable, but it does not entirely explain the disdain some express for this molecule. Perhaps its ability to travel on both sides of the medical road plays a role. How many drugs are able to make you look younger and also help alleviate a wide variety of medical diseases? Only one: Botox. There are no other role models for Botox—nothing else that works well cosmetically and medically. There are no other medicines that can help your migraine headaches, reduce unwanted sweating, help you pee when you want to, help cerebral palsy sufferers, improve your mood, and make you look younger. It sounds a lot like one of those magic tonics sold by traveling salesman at the end of the nineteenth century, but this medicine is real. Let us review some of the many diseases for which Botox is important.

Parkinson's disease (PD) is a complex and progressive movement disorder that can cause symptoms such as tremors, pain, and difficulty with walking and balance. Patients can suffer uncontrollable rigidity in their posture from sustained abnormal activity of their muscles. For example, a PD patient may have a foot that is twisted or pushed down because of a muscle that won't stop working. In addition to pain, this may lead to many falls as a dragged leg gets caught in cracks in a path. To correct this, Botox is injected in a targeted way into the muscles that are distorting the leg, releasing it from the grip of muscle spasms and pain. Within a week of injections, muscle relaxation allows many patients to walk normally again. Botox has been FDA approved to treat PD patients.

Sometimes a PD patient can develop a twisted or tilted neck. Not only is this painful, but it makes it difficult to turn one's head for driving. Botox can help restore the normal neck position, allowing PD patients to continue driving and remain independent.

Similarly, Botox is now approved for cervical dystonia, a condition that causes the neck to twitch, twist, go through repetitive movements, and carry the head in abnormal postures. It happens because involuntary muscle contractions hinder normal movement and cause severe, chronic neck pain.

Cerebral palsy represents another group of movement and muscle disorders that can be helped by Botox injections. Muscle tightness and spasticity caused by the disorder make walking difficult and can worsen over time as muscle spasms increase in severity. Writing can also be difficult. By injecting Botox into the stronger, spastic muscles, the weaker muscles can be strengthened and stretched, and normal movement can be partially restored. Children who were previously bound to wheelchairs have been able to walk. While not a cure for cerebral palsy, Botox injections can dramatically improve the quality of life for young children suffering from this disease.

Sometimes the benefits of botulinum toxin have been discovered by serendipity. An Atlanta plastic surgeon noticed that many of the patients on whom he had used botulinum toxin cosmetically reported back to him that botulinum toxin had not only removed their facial wrinkles but their migraine headaches as well. Word spread quickly, and many doctors began using botulinum toxin "off-label" for headache treatment. Years ago my operating room nurse Sharon suffered from severe and frequent migraines. They weren't hard to recognize. Her head would become slightly tilted, one eye would be bloodshot, and it was easy to see that she was in pain. Botox completely prevented her headaches for three months at a time. As soon as the Botox wore off, the headaches would reemerge, but fortunately, like clockwork, a new round of injections suppressed the migraines.

Migraine headaches were originally thought to be primarily a disorder of blood vessels, but the effective prevention of many a migraine by botulinum toxin has opened a new window into the role that facial and scalp muscles play in the disorder. Few would have predicted that botulinum toxin would become a standard treatment for migraines. But controlled studies have now been done, and Botox is currently FDA approved for injection into the forehead and scalp to treat and prevent migraine headaches.

Botulinum toxin has also been approved for treating underarm sweating. It sounds trivial until you learn that some sufferers sweat so much that they are forced to carry several changes
of clothing with them daily. They can't take their jackets off
without disturbing their coworkers. The excessive sweating is
caused by overstimulation of sweat glands. Botulinum toxin
injection into the armpits quiets the glands responsible for those
drenched shirts. Botulinum toxin is also being used to combat
sweaty palms, which, as any salesman can tell you, are not good
for business.

In some patients with multiple sclerosis or a spinal cord injury,
the bladder may not communicate normally with the brain,
leading to overactive bladder muscles. Instead of filling with
urine and relaxing, the bladder muscles contract, decreasing the
normal volume of urine that the bladder can hold. This leads to
unwanted leakage of urine or urinary incontinence. Injections
of Botox can relax the overactive bladder muscle and have now
been FDA approved for this condition.

The diversity of clinical uses for botulinum toxin will only
increase as we discover more maladies that can be remedied by
treating a specific muscle. Research around the world has led
to the discovery of an ever-expanding list of medical uses for
botulinum toxin, as many disorders are caused by muscles that
contract when they shouldn't or muscles whose use worsens the
disease, and botulinum toxin halts the nerve impulses that fire
the muscle into action.

What is surprising is how many different diseases can be
helped by botulinum toxin. Since botulinum toxin is specific
for its inhibition of muscle contraction, we have learned how

important a role muscles play in different diseases. In addition, for many diseases, muscles provide a suitable entry point for treatment. For example, underarm sweating is not caused by a problem with the tiny muscles around the sweat glands in your armpits. But you need those little muscles to propel your sweat from under your skin to the skin surface. Therefore, if you inhibit those muscles from working, you can no longer sweat in those areas.

Some do not believe in the concept of cosmetic surgery and thus distrust anything that can change one's appearance. But the distinction between reconstructive and aesthetic surgery has always been a blurry one. How does one judge a rhinoplasty that corrects a deviated septum, allowing one to breathe better while simultaneously refining the tip of the nose? The surgery clearly helps breathing, but what pleases the patient more—better breathing or a better profile?

But is more and more of a good thing still good? Like any powerful tool, botulinum toxin can be overused. Every dermatologist has occasionally seen patients look frozen because of the injudicious use of too much botulinum toxin. However, that is definitely not the norm. When used at proper doses and proper injection sites, the effects of botulinum toxin A are more subtle. We need our faces to communicate with others: if you can't move your forehead or your eyebrows, you can't give all those visual cues, mostly unconscious, that help others understand what you're trying to say. For the same reason that most of us would prefer to discuss serious emotional issues in person rather than over the telephone, movement in our faces helps us "talk" to others. Think about all those misunderstandings that begin with casual chatting on the Internet, chatting that deprives one of evaluating all the clues of communication, including the tone and timbre of voice, body posture, and facial expression. The same applies to plastic surgery: we have all seen that face-lift gone awry. There may be an ideal in beauty, but there are many ways to get to Rome, none of which requires casting our faces from the same mold.

CHAPTER 2

LESSONS FROM SALPÊTRIÈRE

"Everything can be taken from a man but one thing: the last of the human freedoms—to choose one's attitude in any given set of circumstances, to choose one's own way."

—Viktor Frankl, *Man's Search for Meaning*

I WAS FIRST compelled to begin research on the relationship between facial expression and mood after my mother's death. She had suffered from depression for years. I became aware of her depression when I went away to summer camp when I was 13. I missed both my parents and was looking forward to their coming up to see me on visiting day. My dad, as always, had a happy look on his face when he gave me a hug. But something was wrong with my mother. She couldn't stop frowning. No matter what she said, her face said something else: she was unhappy. Summer camp represented the beginning of my sister's and my independence from her, which translated into a diminished role for her as caregiver, one of her major sources of self-esteem. She depended on our dependence on her, and our lessening dependence triggered a depression.

As a kid I didn't have the intellectual framework to completely understand what I was witnessing. But the basic features of depression became apparent to me after my summer camp experience. I became steadily more aware of my mother's pain. She hid it well from my sister and me most of the time, though I could read her mood simply by studying her face, which was a window into her world. I remember one Sunday afternoon preparing for my first summer trip to Europe. My father took a picture of my mother and me that day, and years later I came across the photo buried in an old desk drawer. I saw how my mother's frowning face contrasted with my upbeat expression. I began asking myself then whether her constant frowns actually made her depression worse. The more she frowned, it seemed, the greater her suffering. When she was well, her face relaxed.

I learned the full story about my mother's mental health on a cold November night when I was 25. It was dark and rainy, and Mom had been hit by a car when she was crossing the road. I sat in a hospital room listening to an intern take her medical history as she lay in bed with a fractured pelvis, weak from losing several pints of blood. Luckily, she had not hit her head, and her words flowed more freely than usual, most likely because she was anemic and had less oxygen reaching her brain. The doctor was trying to ascertain why she had been hit. Was she depressed, suicidal? She related her history of depression, and I found out that she had first become depressed when her mother had a stroke and required her care. She recovered but became depressed again when I was born—classic post-partum depression. A twinge of guilt passed through me. She went on to claim that she had recovered and was not at all suicidal when that black car ran into her.

Ten years later, after a long struggle with Alzheimer's, my father died, and my mother started a terminal slide into the black hole of depression once more. Medications did not help. As a last resort, she underwent electric convulsive therapy (ECT). For many people it works, but it turned my mother into a helpless, infantile ghost of her former self. She was reduced to a brain-damaged shell of a person who had lost her cherished memories and needed constant care. She died seven years later, her mind in a stuporous haze.

After my mother died, I began to replay her depression in my head, like a movie with a different ending, the way you do sometimes after a traumatic accident when you wonder how things might have turned out if only you had seen it coming sooner. Was my mother's frown more than just a symptom of depression? Did her frowning feed back to her brain or the other way around? As a physician, I had always tried to make sure that my parents got the best that medicine could provide—a sort of sacred duty that a physician son could try to fulfill. But her treatment was wanting. I felt guilty that no one had been able to help her. Sometimes a loss can provide a great incentive for a gain. Was there anything more that I could have done?

WILLIAM JAMES, THE eminent American philosopher and psychologist, wrote in 1890:

> Common-sense says, we lose our fortune, are sorry and weep; we meet a bear, are frightened and run; we are insulted by a rival, are angry and strike. The hypothesis here to be defended says that this order of sequence is incorrect, that the one mental state is not immediately induced by the other, that the bodily manifestations must first be interposed between, and that the more rational statement is that we feel sorry because we cry, angry because we strike, afraid because we tremble, and not that we cry, strike, or tremble, because we are sorry, angry, or fearful, as the case may be.

With his words, James helped introduce the facial feedback hypothesis, the many versions of which converge around the central theme that your facial expressions actively contribute to your emotional state. James continued, "What is equally prominent, but less likely to be admitted until special attention is drawn to the fact, is the continuous cooperation of the voluntary muscles in our emotional states."

While James did not specifically single out the facial muscles for their role in the generation of emotion, it is noteworthy that most of the examples he used to illustrate his hypothesis included some aspect of facial expression. Thus, he asked, "Can one fancy the state of rage and picture no ebullition in the chest, no flushing of the face, no dilatation of the nostrils, no clenching of the teeth?"

If you don't believe James, try sometime to feel really angry about something and, at the same time, smile and laugh as hard as you can. You may have angry thoughts, but your smiling and laughing will make it difficult to "feel" them.

A natural way that many of us think about our emotions is that our perception of some fact triggers our minds to feel an emotion and that this state of mind gives rise to the bodily expression of the emotion. What James was saying is that this common-sense way of viewing our emotions is wrong. Rather, he theorized that "the bodily changes follow directly the perception of the exciting fact, and... our feeling of the same changes as they occur *is* the emotion" (italics original). In other words, without our bodies' ability to express the emotion, it ceases to exist. He goes on: "What kind of an emotion of fear would be left if the feeling neither of quickened heart-beats nor of shallow breathing, neither of trembling lips nor of weakened limbs, neither of goose-flesh nor of visceral stirrings, were present, it is quite impossible for me to think." For James, the vital point of his theory is this: "If we fancy some strong emotion, and then try to abstract from our consciousness of it all the feelings of its bodily symptoms, we find we have nothing left behind." He sums up succinctly: "A purely disembodied human emotion is a nonentity."

But James's theories were unfashionable for much of the twentieth century, in part because of the difficulty of measuring emotions and in part because behaviorism dominated psychology for many years. Early models of how the brain worked were largely inspired by the metaphor of the mind as a computer, a model that downplayed the importance of emotions. For many scientists, the study of emotion appeared to be a minefield with too many difficulties to be considered for serious study—too many difficulties for it to provide a path to tenure in an academic institution. To avoid the problems in studying emotions, researchers took the path of least resistance: they just completely denied their role in our lives. In spite of the obvious power of emotions to affect human behavior, it was more appealing to focus on the part of our brains, the cortex, that helps generate conscious thoughts and helps direct our goal-oriented behavior; the cortex is much more highly developed in humans and helps separate us from all the creatures around us. Emotions link us back to our more primitive ancestors—even reptiles have similar deeper parts of the brain that are involved in emotions—and for most of the twentieth century, we tried to increase

Figure 2.1   Salpêtrière Hospital, 1853 (48 x 56, resin on wood, 2005)

the conceptual distance between us and other organisms. But James's ideas would help set the stage for a more recent resurgence of mechanistic research on emotion.

Around the time that I was reading James's theories, I came across a series of photographs and stories of hysterical, depressed, psychotic female patients treated in the late nineteenth century at the Salpêtrière Hospital in Paris. When you learn about this hospital, you enter a world where science, theater, art, the occult, and hypnotism all swirled around mental illness during its early days of classification and description. The photographs of the facial expressions of the female patients are mesmerizing, and they inspired me to delve deeper and to make paintings about those patients. What role did their faces play in why they were in that hospital?

Long ago Charles Darwin noted, "the insane ought to be studied, for they are liable to the strongest passions, and give uncontrollable vent to them." The pictures we see of inpatients in a nineteenth-century mental hospital do not disappoint.

The Salpêtrière Hospital derives its name from its sixteenth-century origins as an arsenal for gunpowder (which was made from saltpeter). In the seventeenth century, it became a women's hospital, which meant in reality that it was a holding place for female outcasts from society. Part of the grim history of the Salpêtrière includes the massacre of 1792, when a mob attacked the hospital, killing its female occupants. The insane, epileptic, violent, crippled, old, poor, and, for a time, prostitutes and criminals were all thrown together in an institution that Sigmund Freud called the "wilderness of paralyses, spasm and convulsions." The gripping images of Salpêtrière's mentally ill women drew me into a time and place that was really the beginning of the scientific discipline of neurology.

I was fascinated by the pioneering attempts of the Salpêtrière physicians to understand and categorize mental illness. Like doctors today, they used the most advanced tools at their disposal, which included the relatively new medium of photography.

Jean-Martin Charcot, one of the founders of the modern discipline of neurology, was the head physician at Salpêtrière. He is credited with discovering the pathology of amyotrophic lateral sclerosis (ALS), commonly known as Lou Gehrig's disease. He also contributed to our understanding of Parkinson's disease (PD), multiple sclerosis, and neurosyphilis. Hysteria was a common disease in the nineteenth century, and Augustine, a young hysteric who posed for her doctors, became my muse for both a series of paintings and my investigations into the role of facial expressions in emotions and depression.

It's hard to really understand the power that hysteria had in the nineteenth century because today because it has largely disappeared as a disease. It lived on the border between psychosomatic and somatic disease. It is an illness that was much more common in women and is a condition in which the patient exhibits a variety of neurologic symptoms, such as transient paralysis, loss of hearing, and loss of speech, without any organic evidence of disease. The facial expressions of this young hysteric were riveting.

I asked myself: what was going on here? My paintings were based on real photographs of patients in Salpêtrière, but the subjects reminded me more of actors in a play being performed in

Figure 2.2 Augustine in her normal state (36 x 36, epoxy resin on aluminum, 2005)

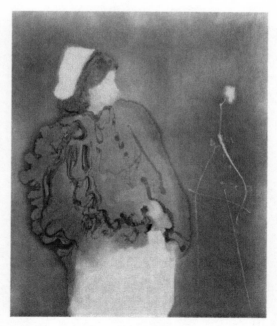

Figure 2.3 Catalepsie provoked by a bright light (48 x39, resin on wood, 2005)

Figure 2.4   Photophobic hysteric (36 x36, resin on aluminum, 2005)

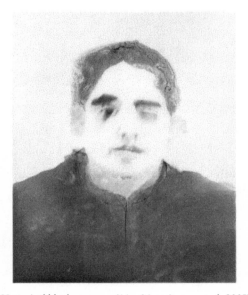

Figure 2.5   Hysterical blepharospasm (44 x 36, resin on wood, 2005)

Figure 2.6   Augustine in a state of ecstasy (48 x 39, resin on wood, 2005)

an avadnt-garde theater. The patient appears at times insane, at other times seductive, coyly acknowledging the viewer. The images shook my concept of a physician. I endeavored to learn more about the main protagonists.

Augustine Gleizes was admitted to the hospital at the age of 16 because of frequent hysterical seizures that left her temporarily paralyzed. While there were no clear anatomical reasons for her seizures, there were plenty of traumatic psychological ones.

At ten she was sexually assaulted by a friend's acquaintance, and at 13 she was raped by her mother's employer. Shortly thereafter she began to have hysterical convulsions. The story worsens when you learn that Augustine found out that her mother had actually sold her to her employer as a sexual favor. After Augustine began to have hysterical fits, her mother eventually brought her to Salpêtrière.

Augustine suffered from frequent hysterical attacks that included hearing voices and having visual hallucinations. To help document her case, the Salpêtrière physicians photographed her and sometimes hypnotized her to have her reenact, when she was well, some of the body positions and facial expressions that occurred during her seizures—sort of like the artist Cindy Sherman posing herself in different roles in front of the camera, except that this was a hospital in 1882.

Figure 2.7 shows Augustine dressed up as a nurse.

In those early days of psychiatry, the separation between the role of a physician as healer and as warden of a mental asylum was not so clear. Patients had no rights whatsoever once they were admitted. Their fate rested solely in the hands of the doctors in charge. And the disease called hysteria, which was characterized by drama, excessive emotionality, hallucinations, temporary paralysis, and fits of convulsions for which no one could find an anatomical cause, became the subject of study by Charcot and his team. Charcot would arrange weekly demonstrations of hysterics acting out. They would be photographed, drawn, and sculpted as a few chosen patients would demonstrate their spectacular forms of disease in front of their doctors and

Figure 2.7   "Catalepsy: Suggestion" (40 x 40, resin on wood, 2005)

the lay public. Charcot understood the power of publicity, and his weekly sessions were a well-attended spectacle. The patients became, in effect, medical celebrities.

Charcot revolutionized the treatment of hysterics by changing the view of hypnosis as quackery. He discovered that hypnosis was a powerful tool that could be used to help relieve hysterics of their symptoms.

After a time, Augustine no longer suffered from spontaneous fits and gradually lost favor in her physicians' eyes. Then, suddenly, she suffered a turn for the worse, became violent, and was put in a cell in a straitjacket. But the daring Augustine, accustomed to dramatizing, on her second attempt succeeded in escaping her confinement, disappearing from history by disguising herself as a man.

These moving Salpêtrière photographs haunted and inspired me. I wanted and needed to understand what their facial expressions meant. Perhaps they could give me more insight into my mother's mental illness. So I began reading authors from the period for some historical context. Medicine, as much as any other field, is influenced by the prevailing wisdom and knowledge of the time. Why were the faces of all these women so mesmerizing? Did their nineteenth-century physicians take more of an interest in the facial expressions of the mentally ill because they understood less of the inner workings of the brain? Were they acting more as natural historians than healers? And were they in some ways more adept because they lacked the medical tools to which we have been accustomed? If you can't order a

Figure 2.8   Andre Brouillet at Salpêtrière (Credit: Erich Lessing, Art Resource, NY)

battery of tests, perhaps you become a better observer of the patient in front of you. No reflexive ordering of brain CAT scans—the physician focused on the patients and their behavior, expressions, and clinical course.

Sigmund Freud was a student of Charcot. In his *Studies on Hysteria*, Freud discusses how a hypnotized patient can remember painful emotional traumas that disappear on awakening. He surmised that the hysterical symptoms were a way to confront emotions so painful that they could not be expressed consciously. Freud had concluded that either a "current sexual conflict or the effect of earlier sexual experiences," such as the physical act of sexual abuse, was the cause of hysteria. This hypothesis appears on target for Augustine and revealed Freud's concept of repression and the power of the unconscious.

When I read Freud's reference to Darwin's writings about emotions in *The Expression of Emotions in Man and Animals*, I took the opportunity to read this classic. In his prescient and ground-breaking book, Darwin states, "The free expression by outward signs of an emotion intensifies it. On the other hand, the repression, as far as this is possible, of all outward signs softens our emotions. He who gives way to violent gestures will increase his rage; he who does not control the signs of fear will experience fear in a greater degree." In other words, like William James, Darwin had reasoned that the physical and outward expression of an emotion is important for its bearer to feel it. He concluded that, "even the simulation of an emotion tends to arouse it in our minds." One hundred years later, psychologists would prove this experimentally.

If you make yourself look sad, Darwin suggested, you may actually feel sad. Conversely, if you express anger in your face, you will feel angrier. And, if you show nothing in your face, the emotion will be diminished. This seems like one of the earliest versions of the facial feedback hypothesis. But if you ask ten people whether they think that by making a certain face they could alter their mood, not many would jump to that conclusion. Somehow Darwin's musings never became part of our popular thinking. Nevertheless, the link that he and James made between facial expression and mood encouraged me to conduct my own investigation.

Could it be that the facial expressions of Augustine, her fellow patients, and my own mother were actually part and parcel of their disease and not just an end result? And what would happen if they couldn't smile or frown? Would that have affected their ability to experience emotions? Maybe abnormal facial expressions and facial muscle activity are not just a reflection of the disease but rather central to and causative of the disease. We are used to thinking of the face as a window into, or a mirror of, our internal states. Perhaps our facial expressions are much more than transient reflections of our inner states; perhaps they are actually the power behind the throne.

Around this time, my wife, a research biochemist, raved about a talk given at the National Institutes of Health by Jonathan Cole, an English neurologist, regarding a patient who could not smile or frown. In his fascinating book *About Face*, Cole explains that the patient, an Anglican priest named James, was born with an inability to use most of his facial muscles because of a rare disorder known as Moebius syndrome. The majority of individuals with Moebius syndrome cannot close their eyes very well or form facial expressions due to a paralysis of the sixth and seventh cranial nerves. Most people with Moebius syndrome have normal intelligence but present with a mask-like appearance.

Cole asked James, "Have you ever felt it is more difficult to experience extreme happiness or sadness or even less obvious transient moods...or have you just dissociated the way in which you view moods from any bodily expression of them?"

"I think there's a lot of dissociation," James replied. "But I do think I get trapped in my mind or my head. I sort of think happy or think sad, not really saying or recognizing actually feeling happy or feeling sad. Perhaps I have had difficulty in recognizing that what I'm putting a name to is not a thought at all but a feeling. Maybe I have to intellectualize mood. I have to say to myself this thought is a happy thought, and therefore I am happy."

James knew his emotions only from a purely Platonic point of view. His story reinforced my growing conviction that facial expressions play an integral role in generating as well as experiencing feelings and moods. You need the movement in your face to help you "feel" the emotion. This is quite an impressive bit of self-analysis by a patient who is unable to properly move his face. In the absence of facial movement, he is forced to deduce that he should be happy because he had a happy thought, and so, logically, he should be happy, even if he can't feel it.

Another individual with Moebius syndrome spoke of interacting with a patient who was visibly sad. "I wasn't able to return it. I tried to do so with words and tone of voice, but it was no use. Stripped of the facial expression, the emotion just dies there, unshared. It just dies." This woman recognized how important her face was for empathy and how her lack of facial movement impeded her ability to show her empathy.

In medicine it is always useful to study the extremes of any characteristic, as this helps us to define the salient features of that trait and how it affects our overall health. Moebius patients are born with difficulty moving their face. But what happens if you lose the ability to make facial expressions later in life? Researchers have discovered that, whether inborn or acquired, the inability to make facial expressions is associated with emotional impairment.

As it turns out, nature has done the experiment for us; the disease is called PD. Patients with PD have difficulty with muscle movement in general and facial expression in particular. Later in their disease, they may present with a "masked" facies, an expressionless face that can cause many difficulties in their interactions with others. They have trouble recognizing the emotions of others as well as experiencing emotions themselves. Of course the disorder involves much more than just the face, but the problems these patients encounter is instructive. They have difficulty making decisions, which is probably related to their decreased emotional responsiveness. (Our emotions are critical in making quick decisions.)

Here is how one Parkinson's patient describes his struggle with the disease:

> Much of the sense of what we all say is not in the voice or words, but in the subtle visual cues and signals the face sends.

We all interpret speech in the light of what we read in a person's expression. People with Parkinson's can slowly lose the ability to enhance communication this way without even knowing it.

Think about the problem of misinterpretation of e-mail. The sender composes a message in which the words seem clear as the send button is pushed.

The recipient looks at the cold, expressionless type on their screen, and without the guidance of the visual and tone cues that we all use to correctly interpret meaning, assigns meaning that isn't there. Often the missing meaning is misread, and the interpretation negative.

Then consider the way we get around this problem. We insert little faces that clarify our intent ;-)

This is exactly what those of us with Parkinson's disease are not doing in face-to-face conversation. We are sending spoken email, without the emoticons :-(

Instead of this :-) , or this :-(, what we send is this :-| . Nothing but :-|

To complicate things further, we are often unaware that we are not sending the proper cues. And worse, as people look for these cues and cannot find them, they get frustrated, confused and eventually angry.

This incisive writing by a man suffering from PD underscores the importance of our facial expressions for normal social interactions. If you lose the ability to move your face, others may misread your intentions. And often, the misinterpretation is negative, generating mistrust. We are so hardwired to participate in a facial dialogue with others that the absence of this dialogue is alarming. Our minds find it strange and threatening when a fellow human face appears dead in its expression. It is hard to predict what someone with a masked facial expression is going to do next. And that is worrying because we can't rule out danger.

Without the give and take of facial signals, our unconscious is disturbed by the absence of communication with the person standing in front of us. We may not understand why we are disturbed, but it happens nonetheless through unconscious mental processes that we are beginning to untangle.

But in addition to creating misunderstandings between PD patients and others, the disease also impairs emotional understanding in oneself. It is possible that faulty internal communication is an even bigger problem than external communication. With words you can tell someone that you love them, that you have deep feelings for them. But how do you communicate to yourself if a vital communication link is absent? PD patients have trouble recognizing emotions in themselves, impairing their ability to make decisions. Throughout this book we shall discover why our emotions are so important to ourselves, to help us navigate through the innumerable situations that life presents. Your face speaks not just to others but to yourself. And the power of internal communication is not to be underestimated.

CHAPTER 3

FACIAL EXPRESSIONS

"Hearty laughter is a good way to jog internally without having to go outside."

—Norman Cousins

WHY ARE OUR faces so expressive? Perhaps it is because sociality is a defining feature of what it means to be a human. We have had millions of years to evolve our complex and interwoven layers of social intelligence. Although the circumstances of human life have altered dramatically in the past 10,000 years, our nature has not. We are descended from ancient bands of humans whose social skills helped us to prosper and dominate the world. The face, and all the nuances of facial expression, helped tribes of humans work together as teams long before they could speak in sentences. Imagine an ancient hunt for large prey. Sound would give one away—but the glances exchanged between members of a group of hunters could silently provide signals about what to do next, leading to a successful hunt.

If you reflect on all the subtleties of human relationships and the need for the calibration of your response to your fellow human, the privileged role of facial expressions for our behavior makes sense. We needed ways of fine-tuning the different interactions between members of the tribe, from domination to submission, from cooperation to reciprocity, from approval to dislike, to love, anger, fear, disgust, and happiness. We could measure the emotions and intentions of friend and foe alike, helping us avoid unnecessary conflicts, while strengthening bonds and carefully choosing our battles. The face provided a real-time window into the feelings of your fellow humans at a time when they could not express them in words. And by re-creating on your face the expression of the human next to you, your brain could create some of the same emotions they were feeling, facilitating empathy and compassion. Anything that could install loyalty and a sense of belonging could powerfully influence the survival of a band of humans. In the same way that a team of good and cooperative players can beat a team of great but selfish basketball players, so too would reciprocity and understanding between members of a tribe help its success. We are often amazed that a poor sports team can ever match one that overspends it by many millions, but when it happens, it reinforces the power of teamwork.

As with anything that works really well, the underpinnings of facial expression are well hidden from view. When we sit down with a friend over lunch, our faces become active participants in the conversation, usually without either party's becoming consciously aware of it. There are literally thousands of facial movements, varying in intensity and meaning, that are recruited during a one-hour lunch. It helps to slow things down to really appreciate this. Try watching your favorite DVD and slowing down a scene with two actors. Their faces move so much, with expressions that may last only a fraction of a second before transitioning to another expression, each expression punctuating, complementing, embellishing, and commenting on whatever is said with words. Language tells only a part of the story. The nonverbal communication is probably at least as important as any words that are uttered. And the face is the privileged expresser of emotion. Although our bodies and their posture give much information about us, it is less specific than that given by the face. Only the face can give you a clear and precise signal system for emotions. You may be able to tell from body posture that someone is upset, but not whether they are angry, fearful, sad, or disgusted. Yet psychologists can look at videotapes of couples and, by analyzing their facial expressions, predict with good accuracy which unions will last and which will dissolve. Their faces speak volumes, but most is unconscious, and much occurs so quickly that only a careful researcher can decipher what is really there.

If you want to learn more about the dynamic features of the face, spend time with teenagers. For starters, the teenage years are a time of heightened emotions, joys, passions, and sensitivity. Also, the contrast between the smooth contours of fresh, undamaged teenage skin and the creases, furrows, and lines so fleetingly created on it could not be greater. No matter how troubled teenagers' young lives may have been, their faces haven't yet been permanently etched with the lines, wrinkles, and furrows that most of us have aplenty by the time we are middle-aged. Their faces do not yet show the signs of sun damage that can distract us from dynamic expressions. The youthful face is a tabula rasa, a freshly scrubbed chalkboard that displays every new feeling clearly.

I remember sitting with my teenage daughter as she asked whether she could go to a concert on a Tuesday night during a school week. Her voice was hoarse and raspy from a cold she was just beginning to shake off. I knew that staying out late was not about to help her fight this bug. So I said no. Long before words reached her mouth, her forehead told me her thoughts. There was no denying it. Her smooth forehead skin creased immediately, showing me a potent frown, a symbol of her displeasure. But when I asked her at a later time to frown for me, she couldn't do it on command—only her unconscious knew the right path.

My unconscious understood her unconscious long before our conscious minds met on the playing field of words. It's so easy to forget that most of our mental activity occurs in what is called the cognitive unconscious. Almost everything we do is guided by unconscious brain power. If we had to weigh up every action with the scale of our cortex, the outer covering of our brains that enables our conscious thoughts, then life would slow down dramatically. Imagine having to try and calculate exactly how much to contract the quadriceps in order to move one leg in front of another, as in walking. It might take a few hours and a few engineers to figure out just how to walk across the room. Or imagine having to calculate how many tears to shed on hearing of the loss of a loved one. Life as we know it would stop.

SOMETIMES WHEN YOU get up and read the newspaper, you come to the conclusion that humans don't know how to get along with one another. But contrary to what one might assume based on the number of ongoing conflicts around the world, our preverbal hominid ancestors were good at cooperation. They had to be to survive in a world with highly specialized predators who could physically outperform any one of them. Only by employing their superior intelligence and tool-using ability in a group setting could they be successful. Imagine when a group of hominids returned to their homes with captured prey. Suppose the individual who tracked but did not capture the prey received less than his female partner thought their family was due. Lacking words as tools, this preverbal hominid might have expressed her displeasure by frowning at the one dividing up the food. Her message could be easily interpreted, and their share might be increased without conflict emerging. The frown was an early and a successful form of communication. Since ancient hominids survived poorly alone, they needed quick ways to communicate with one another to maintain friendly relations within the group. Before symbolic language evolved, what better way than to smile to signal your happiness with another? Or frown to express your anger? Before words helped us conceptualize our thoughts and feelings, we could communicate in a fraction of a second by moving our lips or eyebrows.

Our emotions have evolved to help us navigate our way through a complex and demanding world. They help us deal with the myriad scenarios that have replayed themselves over eons, from escaping predators to bonding with compatriots, fighting, falling in love, and confronting infidelity. Our faces play a huge role in both feeling and expressing those emotions.

ONE CAN TRACE the evolutionary origins of the muscles of facial expression back to primitive primates.

The most primitive primates, the prosimians, such as lemurs and bush-babies, are nocturnal and have poorly developed vision. They rely mostly on smell, sound, and touch to keep track of their surroundings. It is not surprising that they employ relatively few facial expressions.

By contrast, Old World monkeys have keen vision, essential for their effortless and graceful leaps through trees. Fewer of their facial muscles are devoted to smell, hearing, and touch. At the same time, there is an increase in the size and number of mid-face muscles, resulting in a more mobile mouth and cheek. These social monkeys are more facially expressive than their prosimian counterparts, who come together only to mate. The ability to express a wide range of emotional states should be valuable to Old World monkeys, who live together in groups.

The fundamental evolutionary importance of facial expressions showing our emotional states is seen in the similarity of emotional states described for apes and humans. Apes have been shown to express anger, sadness, and laughter with facial movements that have functional and formal similarities to those of humans. Humans have continued this evolutionary trend with the development of even more finely differentiated facial muscles, which allow for more subtle distinctions between emotional states.

The corrugators, the muscles that help pull the eyebrows together, have become much more developed in humans than in apes. They contract to help the eye shut quickly and fully to prevent damage from something entering or hitting it. The corrugators also help effect the lowering and contraction of the eyebrows to shade against too strong a light, which was most helpful when our ancestors began to hold their heads erect. The corrugators also became more highly developed in humans as they aided in seeing distance objects, as in our squint. While the physical benefits of having strong corrugator muscles are logical, the emotional benefits were probably more important for our evolutionary development. Our facial muscles help to generate our emotional states in addition to their more obvious role in the evolution of communication between humans. And regulation of our emotions was critical to the survival of small groups of humans. The emotions that an early human felt could quickly alert one to safety or danger of any encounter.

DARWIN WAS THE first to propose that human facial expressions are innate and understood by all cultures. He stated "that all the chief expressions exhibited by man are the same throughout the world. This fact is interesting, as it affords a new argument in favor of the several races being descended from a single parent stock." Darwin was remarkably able to transcend the standard prejudice of the time. This is an anti-racist statement, made when racism reigned supreme. Western civilization firmly believed itself to be the summit of human accomplishment. Humans from other societies, including those who had been developing culturally longer than the West, were considered vastly inferior. And here is Darwin, living in a society that considered itself the pinnacle of civilization, recognizing that he is descended from the same ancestor of all humans, regardless of race or tribe.

Darwin concluded that human emotional states were essential for our welfare, for communication between mother and child, for empathy between humans, and for revealing the thoughts and intentions of others more truly than words. He recognized the fundamental facial expressions of happiness, anger, fear, disgust, sadness, and surprise. He studied the emotional expression in animals to argue for the evolutionary origins of our facial expressions. To help support his theories, he described emotional expressions in cats, dogs, horses, nonhuman primates, infants, adults from cultures around the world, the mentally ill, and the blind. And when he first published his work, it was a best seller.

But Darwin's work on facial expression and emotion was largely ignored or dismissed for the next hundred years. A hundred years is a long time for resurrection in science. Usually when scientific work is ignored for a century, it is never revisited. Much scientific work disappears from view within a few years as researchers focus on the most up-to-date and accurate experiments. Darwin's work on facial expressions is a rare exception.

There are several possible reasons that little research on emotion was conducted until the 1960s. Perhaps the largely anecdotal nature of Darwin's observations diminished their importance as the focus on scientific experiments that could be replicated, quantified, and intensified. Darwin also stressed the innate nature of facial expressions; this went against the prevailing dogma of psychologists in the early and mid-twentieth century, which rejected the notion that genetically inheritable characteristics controlled human behavior. Both psychologists and anthropologists had concluded that human behavior in general and facial expressions in particular were learned according to cultural tradition. Accepting that some human behaviors were genetic was unpopular because this theory implied that all humans might not be as equally endowed as they hoped, that perhaps not all humans could be made equal even if their environments were equally benevolent and stimulating. It also drew human behavior closer to other animals, toppling us from the pedestal on which we like to place ourselves. And, of course, such a view was sure to draw the wrath of those who refused to accept our evolutionary origins.

Finally, many were proud to control or even deny emotion, as if that made them more civilized, more rational. The human brain was assumed to operate according to the machine model of logical decision making. From the ancient Greeks to the eighteenth-century German Immanuel Kant, many philosophers have stressed the need to exclude the emotions in order to make intelligent, well-thought-out decisions. We were supposed to suppress our emotions so that we could think more clearly. Men congratulated themselves for not shedding a tear in public, for not displaying their inner feelings. Freud, who was also a keen reader of Darwin, was decidedly alone when he suggested that just the opposite was true—that emotions unconsciously influence many of our decisions, and that emotion and rational reasoning are inseparable. But only recently has the importance of evolutionarily older parts of the brain involved in the generation of emotions been found to play such an important role in our thinking. Without emotions we are inefficient at deciding how to proceed—emotions help us assign value or salience to choice. Without emotion, decision making can become an arduous task. Those unlucky souls who have had the emotion centers of the brain damaged through trauma or disease are unable to successfully navigate their way through this world. Without their emotions, they can't make the simplest of decisions. They get paralyzed just trying to decide between the types of cereal on the supermarket shelf. In addition, the unconscious, emotional part of our brain is much faster to react to potential danger. Long before you have figured out why that loud noise was a gunshot, your body has begun mobilizing to get away from the next volley.

One of the questions that helped rekindle research on emotion was the debate about facial expressions—were they learned or inherited? In the 1960s, many anthropologists thought that facial expressions were unique to each individual culture, just as different languages evolved with their own unique inflections and vocabularies. The connection among the mind, emotions, and facial expression would be much more convoluted and less innate if widely separated human populations had their own facial code. One could imagine the difficulties in declaring fundamental properties of facial movements if Asians used one set of expressions, Africans another, and Western Europeans a third.

To try and solve this question, Paul Ekman and his colleagues showed photographs of people with characteristic facial expressions to college students in five different countries. They asked them to choose one word from a list describing emotions that best fit with the photograph. Whether they were living in Japan, Chile, Argentina, Brazil, or the United States, students identified the same emotional meaning of facial expressions. Nevertheless, many prominent anthropologists still refused to concede that this demonstrated that facial expressions were universal and meant the same thing in all human cultures. Ray Birdwhistell at the University of Pennsylvania contended that Ekman's work demonstrated only that students all over the world had been indoctrinated culturally by the global media through television, movies, and photographs to interpret faces the same way.

To address these criticisms of his results, Ekman searched the world for a people who had never seen a photograph, a television show, or a movie. Even in the late 1960s, there weren't too many people left who filled the bill. Finally he found them in remote areas of New Guinea, where he traveled to repeat his experiments. These tribal people could not read any language and represented the few remaining humans who were visually isolated from all media. (I would expect that one would have extreme difficulty finding subjects with whom to repeat this experiment in today's globalized world.) Ekman's hard work paid off. He was able to show that New Guineans could instinctively recognize the same emotions expressed by a human face as could their university counterparts, thereby confirming the universality of facial expressions. Anger, sadness, fear, disgust, surprise, and happiness were expressed and understood universally, implying that they played a fundamental role in our evolution. Happiness represents the positive pole, attracting you to engage more, while fear, anger, disgust, and sadness are negative emotions that most of us do not enjoy, pushing us away. Surprise may be either positive or negative, depending on whether it is combined with happiness, when you've just seen your long-lost brother, or with terror, when you are surprised and fearful to see that man pointing a gun at you. Most facial expressions can be blended with one another, so that one can be sad and disgusted, or sad and angry, or sad and surprised. It is no wonder that it took so long to decipher facial expressions since they can be combined to encode many nuances of meaning.

Anything so innate must serve an important purpose, akin to the importance of the laws of thermodynamics and gravity, so the field of facial expression and emotions was reborn. It was no longer detrimental to one's academic career to study human emotion and facial expressions.

A recent study takes a different approach to demonstrate the universality and the hardwired nature of facial expression. Researchers compared the facial expressions of blind and sighted judo athletes at Olympic and Paralympic Games. They studied the faces of gold versus silver medal winners. The gold medal winners showed genuine joy, a smile with the mouth and eyes, while the losers displayed fake or "social" smiles that only involved the mouth. The blind athletes showed the same expressions as sighted ones after winning or losing, reinforcing the conclusion that these expressions are innate. Figure 3.1 shows the sad face of a blind athlete after losing an important game. Her facial expression is instantly recognizable by those of us who are sighted.

Three emotions—anger, fear, and sadness—are closely associated with contraction of the corrugator, the muscle that pulls the eyebrows together and creates the frown. We frown with anger and sadness, but the frown can also be simply an expression of surprise or disbelief. What are you talking about? You may also frown if you are puzzled, if something is difficult, such as a math problem. As Darwin wrote in *The Expression of Emotion in Man and Animals* in 1872, "A man may be absorbed in the deepest thought, and his brow will remain smooth until he encounters some obstacle in his train of reasoning, or is interrupted by some disturbance, and then a frown passes like a shadow over his brow. A half-starved man may think intently how to obtain food, but he probably will not frown unless he encounters either in thought or action some difficulty, or finds the food when obtained nauseous." So one meaning of a frown is to express displeasure or difficulty. But if you are sitting all by yourself reading, when that frown passes like a wave over your brow, it is not at all clear to whom that frown is talking. Unless you admit that maybe that frown is talking to its wearer.

Part of the trouble in understanding facial expressions stems from the many distinct roles they play. Over millions of years of evolution they assumed numerous functions. One major one is to tell others what we are thinking and feeling. The way you can look at someone on the street and know that you need to cross to the other side. The way you can see the expression of someone who is crazy and have that immediate gut feeling that you need to move away. Here our faces give us away as they silently talk to those around us. As our faces move, they can forecast to others what our intentions are. Another role is to provide commentary to those around you about what is occurring. Suppose your friend tells you a sad story about her cat. You briefly make a little sad expression with your eyebrows to show her that you empathize with the loss of her favorite feline. By momentarily displaying sadness on your face, you are commiserating with her. She knows you do not feel sad but rather that you understand her sadness.

Sometimes our faces do a good job of talking to others. I had such an experience in college when I walked into our off-campus house in West Philadelphia tired and hungry. I was feeling harassed from the extra course work I was taking that fall semester. Midterm exams loomed. After a long hard day of lectures, laboratory work, and studying in the library, I was fondly anticipating the moment when I could sit down and eat my favorite spaghetti dish (I was a spaghetti nut at school!). Just before I took my first bite, I noticed that my roommate Steven seemed much happier than usual. As the spaghetti entered my mouth, my tongue recoiled from the taste of brine. It was saltier than a sardine. The instant my roommate started giggling, a wave of anger came over me as I realized that he had dumped salt onto my meal. I stood up glowering and advanced on my smaller roommate to do what instinct was telling me to do. Fortunately, before anything happened, another roommate saw the fury in my face and defused the situation with his words. Later he recalled, "Your face was so angry, I was really worried for him."

My angry face clearly told others what I was feeling and warned them about my potential actions. And my frown did an excellent job of that as everyone in the room understood me without words. But in addition to communicating to others, my angry face was playing another role at the same time. What was this less obvious role?

Could I have felt so angry if I hadn't looked angry? I doubt it. My face wasn't just forecasting my bad intentions; my angry look actually contributed to my anger. My angry facial expression was talking *to me,* making *me* feel angrier, raising *my* blood pressure, and tensing *my* muscles to prepare me for a fight. My face was an integral part of a coordinated response that affected my entire being.

Psychologists have been attempting to understand these different roles for years. Much of the debate about facial expressions has probably resulted from our desire to assign one role when there are clearly multiple roles. In addition, each culture does have its own rules for what is socially acceptable to display to others. Therefore, you may see more or less of certain expressions in different cultures. But they are understood well by all. For example, when Japanese and American college students saw a revolting film, they both expressed disgust on their faces when alone; but in the presence of another person, the Japanese masked their negative emotions more than did the Americans. It is not socially acceptable in Japan to show disgust in public. Similarly, in America, bridegrooms infrequently cry at their own weddings, but brides commonly do since there are different rules for male and female behavior in public.

It is clear that the face can predict to others what someone will do next. Like a switch on a railroad track that controls the path of a train, our facial movements affect the course of social interactions, but at the same time they also speak to ourselves, relaying back to our brains a real-time assessment of what is happening emotionally.

As my spaghetti story demonstrates, our facial expressions provide many clues about our deepest thoughts and feelings. But unless you train yourself to really understand facial movement, as Paul Ekman has done, few of us realize that there is a whole world of activity happening with the face all the time, happening so quickly that usually only our unconscious is aware of it. Some of these facial expressions last only for microseconds, long enough to record on video but otherwise difficult to consciously untangle the meaning of all these expressions in real time. It's sort of like the drop of water from your pond in the backyard: without a microscope, you would never be aware of the fantastic variety of life zooming around in the water.

I had my first direct experience with these micro-expressions a few years ago after a long interview with Susan R. She was an attractive and seemingly pleasant young woman applying for a job to work as a physician's assistant in my office. Her face was animated and smiling most of the time. At least it appeared so initially. I asked her why she thought dermatology was right for her. Her past experience had been working in the neonatal intensive care unit of a large hospital, taking care of very ill premature babies—about as different from outpatient dermatology as one could get. As she spoke, my gut began to tell me that something wasn't quite right. She had never worked in dermatology, so it was going to take some convincing for me to be sure that my specialty was a good match for her. I probed deeper. I asked her what personal experiences made her so sure that outpatient dermatology was perfect for her. She smiled and laughed pleasantly while answering, but something about her facial expressions was really bothering me. I couldn't put my finger on it as I left the office that day wondering what was wrong.

That night I dreamt about our interview. Somehow the entire interview was now slowed down enough for me to visualize her fleeting mouth grimaces. They were brief but powerful unconscious demonstrations of annoyance, discontent, and frustration. Susan was upset that I kept on asking questions that she could not answer, so she responded subliminally with conflicted and negative facial expressions. I can only assume that my "gut" feeling was my unconscious registering all those fleeting but angry faces. When I awoke from my dream, I had flashbacks to the bizarre contortions that her mouth had undergone. It was only when my mind revisited the memories that they slowed down enough for me to fully recognize these unconscious grimaces for what they really were—anger directed toward me for asking probing questions that she could not answer.

We now understand that these brief *micro-expressions* represented emotions that Susan was trying to suppress, emotions that leaked out but were repressed so quickly that I could not consciously see them. These expressions lasted well under a second, sometimes as briefly as 1/25th of a second. She was upset with me but did not permit herself to show it consciously; however, her angry thoughts were unconsciously being expressed on her face nonetheless. Unless we are highly trained in the art of deception or are a skilled actor, most us will show true clues on our faces that a good student of facial expressions can interpret correctly. Paul Ekman has discovered enough of the science behind this that it is now taught to law-enforcement officials to help detect deceit.

CHAPTER 4

THE MUSCLE OF JOY

"A smile cures the wounding of a frown."

—Shakespeare

ONE DAY ON a trip to New York City, I entered the subway
and heard an Asian man passionately playing his erdhu, a
simply built Chinese string instrument, in a duet with an accordion played by a Russian in a Siberian hat. China and Russia
meeting in a gray, noisy, crowded train cellar in America—and
I wasn't the only one who was enchanted. A steady stream of
commuters, normally unmoved by anything during their dazed,
somnambulistic journey to work, walked over to pay tribute to
the unlikely duo by dropping money into the accordion player's
open instrument case. Both musicians continued playing their
music passionately, gently moving their faces to mirror their
music, but not the expressions of the commuters around them.
Suddenly, a small boy, no more than five or six, darted in front
of the musicians to drop a penny into their kitty. The boy turned
quickly and never saw the beam of the accordionist's warm,

long, gentle smile of delight. His face had been weathered by the thousand makeshift stages he had played on. Yet he was moved by this most genuine of gestures, from a child, from a stranger, a gesture made more poignant by the age of its owner.

Why did the accordion player smile? It all happened so quickly that he didn't have time to "think" about it. And the boy could no longer see him, so who was the accordion player smiling at? His utter delight with this generous act by a small child engendered his smile. Like most of our facial expressions, the accordionist's smile involved no conscious input. His smile represented the positive pole of a circuit of emotions connected with facial expressions.

We have seen so many smiles in our lifetime (one hopes that is true!) that we don't often reflect on this ubiquitous facial expression. Most of the time it just happens—no planning is necessary. We smile at others to express our pleasure with their actions or their words. An honest smile defuses hostility and pulls others closer to us. The ability of a smile to inform others of our good intentions, of our happiness, is one of its important roles. As a social signal, the smile is universally recognized. Even if you can't speak the native tongue, as a traveler you can instantly make friends by smiling. "If you smile at me, I will understand," sings Stephen Stills. "'Cause that is something everybody everywhere does in the same language." Stills may not have read Darwin, but he instinctively knew that he was right.

Why do we like smiles? A smile tells us that things are good, that we can let our guard down, that we will not be attacked by the man smiling at us. Not only that, but the region of the brain that is activated by reward and thought to be the locus of pleasure in the brain is activated by seeing a smiling face and even more by the act of smiling. When we see a beautiful face, the same area is also activated. The very act of looking at a smiling face makes us feel better. By stimulating these positive emotions, we feel comfortable approaching this fellow human and developing the relationship. We smile to others to signal back to them that, yes, we understood their smile and we are on the same wavelength. Ultimately, the reciprocal nature of facial expressions contributes enormously to empathy. The urge to smile back at the one who smiled at us is strong.

What is really amazing is that just by looking at someone smiling, even briefly, we stimulate our own smile muscle to contract a little bit. Smiling prompts mimicry and raises the emotional state of all who observe it. This is how empathy works. It is also one reason that we like to spend time with jovial people. They elevate our mood. This is all hardwired in our brains to help us understand what the face of our friend next to us is really saying. Edgar Allan Poe intuited long ago the knowledge that one can gain by mimicking the facial expressions of our fellow humans. In 1844, Poe described how the human face could generate emotional experiences and how the simple act of changing one's facial features could alter how one thought and felt. He did this through Auguste Dupin, his detective hero in *The Purloined Letter*, who informs the reader how he learned how to solve murder mysteries from a card-playing child champion, who said, "When I wish to find out how wise or how stupid or how good or how wicked is anyone or what are his thoughts at the moment, I fashion the expression of my face, as accurately as possible, in accordance with the expression of his, and then wait to see what thoughts or sentiments arise in my mind or heart, as if to match or correspond with the expression."

This mimicry of facial expressions around us is completely unconscious. We are fundamentally literal beings in terms of how our brains work—so if you want to understand your friend's emotions, your face re-creates a much diminished version, not visible to those around us, but sending enough signals back to our brains that we understand their feelings. If we see a happy, sad, or fearful face, we activate the same neural networks as when we experience happiness, sadness, or fear ourselves. The empathic response is weaker than the emotions of the person we view—but it informs us what they are experiencing, and this greatly facilitates our social communication, our bonding. We certainly smile to communicate with our brethren, but that is not all; just watch a friend who is reading silently, alone in his study, display a huge grin on discovering a humorous passage. He would have smiled regardless of whether he knew of your presence.

One of the most crucial roles of smiling, to make the owner of the smile happier, is under-recognized. Your smile speaks to you as much as to anyone around you. How does your brain decide how happy you are? One way is your unconscious monitoring of your own smile muscle—if it is active, your brain receives reports of the good news, boosting your conscious mood. If you spend all day having fun with your friends, smiling away, you will feel better, and your smile will have played a large part.

The importance of the smile is underscored by the most famous painting in history, which also shows the most enigmatic smile. Some years after Leonardo painted the *Mona Lisa*, Giorgio Vasari, the Italian Renaissance artist and author, wrote that the artist "employed singers and musicians and jesters to keep her full of merriment and so chase away the melancholy that painters usually give to portraits." No doubt this is an apocryphal story, but it sets the stage for Vasari's next comment. In this painting, "there was a smile so pleasing that it seemed divine rather than human; and those who saw it were amazed to find that it was as alive as the original."

Vasari was definitely tapping into the magic of this painting that has captivated so many. Why does Leonardo's masterpiece have such power? Perhaps it is because Mona Lisa's expression is cloaked in mystery that is simply indefinable—her subtlety intrigues us as it draws us in, but it keeps us wandering in the picture, searching for a definite conclusion. Her enigmatic lip position hints at, but does not disclose, the emotions within her. Smile lines are normally generated around the mouth and sometimes the eyes. But Mona Lisa has soft shadows instead of lines around her eyes and mouth. Shadows without lines are anatomically impossible. And therein lies the magic of the painting. Her eyes seem to be smiling, though the longer you look, the less sure you are. The painting shows the power of a facial expression to captivate us. As our minds try to understand this painting by unconsciously re-creating Mona Lisa's expression in our own facial muscles, we are thoroughly confused, and there is nothing like ambiguity to hold our attention.

I wonder what facial expression Leonardo would have made on learning what the founder of psychoanalysis thought about his painting. Freud was captivated enough by this painting to try to psychoanalyze it and its maker. He believed that because Leonardo was born out of wedlock and spent his early years with his unmarried mother, she would have overindulged him. Freud said, "When in the prime of life, Leonardo once more encountered the smile of bliss and rapture which once played on his mother's lips as she fondled him." To Freud, Mona Lisa's smile was a sign of Leonardo da Vinci's Oedipal love for his mother.

What really happens when we smile? The neuronal signals for smiles usually start in the outer covering of the brain, the cortex, and from there they travel to the deeper part of the brain, the brainstem, which, in terms of evolution, also happens to be one of the oldest parts of our brain. Then connections are made to an even more ancient part of the brain called the pons and, finally, to a special region from which a visible nerve, called the seventh cranial nerve, emerges in front of the ear. This nerve travels from its deep origin until it rises to a more central part of the face, where it reaches the smile muscle, which is buried under the skin. The smile muscle is attached from the mouth to the cheekbone. When this nerve fires off, the smile muscle is activated, the corners of our mouth are pulled up, and we look happy. And if it is a true smile, one that signifies real enjoyment by its wearer, then a branch of the facial nerve also activates those little muscles around the eyes, leading to wrinkling around the eyes in addition to a mouth smile (Figure 4.1).

The scientific analysis of the smile really began with the French anatomist Guillaume-Benjamin-Amand Duchenne de Boulogne. In the 1860s, he used electrical currents to make

Figure 4.1   Mouth and eye, Duchenne, smile

his subjects' "facial muscles contract to speak the language of the emotions and the sentiments." Duchenne believed that one could gain insight into the ways the face expresses emotions by studying the muscles underlying facial movement. He recorded the expressions produced by the electrical stimulation by taking photographs and was the first to use photography to prove a scientific theory. Duchenne showed that in the particular smile he called the "smile of joy," the muscle that is just to the side of the eyes (orbicularis oculi) is activated. When this muscle contracts, it creates creases, sometimes called crow's feet. He called this the "true smile," the pure smile of enjoyment. Duchenne concluded that the mouth smile obeys the will, but the eye smile does not. He said, "The muscle around the eye...is only brought into play by a true feeling, an agreeable emotion. Its inertia in smiling unmasks a false friend."

In Figure 4.2, Duchenne applies electrodes to his cooperative subject in order to stimulate the contraction of the smile muscle (zygomaticus major) that pulls the corners of the mouth up when we smile. His subject is clearly enjoying this. Duchenne's jolt of electricity activates the smile muscle around the mouth,

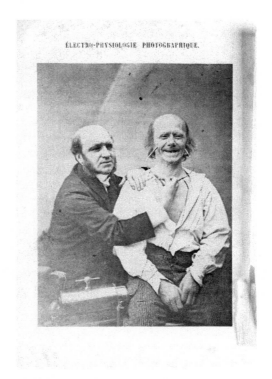

ÉLECTRO-PHYSIOLOGIE PHOTOGRAPHIQUE.

Figure 4.2   Duchenne de Boulougne stimulating smile muscle

but the gentleman's eyes are also smiling, as seen by the creases formed just to the side of his eyes so the happiness comes from inside. When Duchenne first applied the electricity, only the smile muscle around the mouth was activated; he realized that it didn't look like a true, natural smile, so he told this gentleman a joke to make his eyes smile as well.

Paul Ekman, who led the scientific investigation of facial expressions in the twentieth century, has shown that Duchenne was right. Few of us can fake an eye smile. If you're sitting across from a new business associate and he smiles at you but you're still not sure if you should sign off on a new business venture, look at those little lines around the outside of his eyes. If they wrinkle up like crow's feet, then his smile is a real signifier of pleasure or happiness. The absence of smiling eyes should alert you that your new associate's smile is not necessarily as friendly as it looks.

A century after Duchenne recorded his remarkable experiments, Dr. Paul Ekman honored the anatomist by terming the smile involving the eyes the "Duchenne smile." Ekman found that the failure to distinguish between different types of smiles showed up in much scientific research over the years and might explain contradictory findings regarding the universal meaning of the smile. Other scientists confirmed their findings and found that the Duchenne smile appears significantly more often when people are freely enjoying themselves than in situations that would require feigned smiles. The eyes do not lie unless, of course, the person has received Botox around the eyes, in which case the skin around the eyes is unable to wrinkle up, no matter how true a smile.

How important is a smile in our evaluation of others? More influential than one might suspect. When college students were asked to attribute characteristics to anonymous photos, they overwhelmingly judged smiling faces to be more sincere, sociable, and competent! No wonder then that the last hundred years of advertising has emphasized the smile. If you want to sell anything, sell it on the promise of delight, the promise of happiness. Even if the ad is selling some test to detect narrowing of the carotid artery in your neck or a cancer in the lung, the older couple is always smiling!

Certainly what we see greatly influences when we smile, but it is not necessary. We need no visual feedback to smile. Darwin discovered that those who are born blind will still smile appropriately during a conversation. You can smile when all alone, but smiling is definitely enhanced by socializing; it happens six times more frequently in social settings.

Some of the complexities of smiling can be appreciated by examining those who can't do it normally. People who have suffered brain damage may not be able to smile when asked to but will still involuntarily smile at a joke. Conversely, patients suffering from PD, a disease of dopamine-containing neurons in the brain, may be able to turn up the corners of the mouth when asked to smile but after getting a joke may lack the ability to smile as a natural, automatic response. Patients who have had a stroke leading to paralysis of half of their face lack an ability to voluntarily move one side of their face. They show a crooked smile when asked to grin but a normal smile on hearing a joke, indicating intact nerve pathways beyond their conscious control. Clearly, the pathways for smiling are quite elaborate, with both unconscious and conscious connections that receive inputs from different parts of the brain.

We have learned how smiling activates the part of the brain that gets more active when we are happy. One wonders whether it is only a coincidence that those of us who socialize the most tend to get less depressed. We have seen how socializing is a great activator of smiling—perhaps smiling is doing more than we think. Do children suffer less often from depression because they spend more time playing and smiling? It is so easy to forget that your face is always speaking to you: 24/7, your brain is keeping track of how many smiles you created with your face. Your smile scorecard is not something you are consciously aware of, but your unconscious has intimate knowledge of it. I believe that smiling more benefits you directly—even without its social benefits. You go to the gym to strengthen your muscles. Why not go to the smiling gym to strengthen your positive emotions?

One study found that women who had smiled the most in their college yearbook photos had happier lives, happier marriages, and fewer personal setbacks in the following 30 years. Another study finds a correlation between how big a smile you made for a baseball card photo and how long you will live. Those baseball players who had the broadest smiles lived, on average, seven years longer than those who smiled the least.

How could smiling lead to happier marriages and longer lives? The key is probably the reduction of stress that your body and mind feel. Smiling helps generate positive happy emotions within you, and this leads to a decrease in the stress-induced hormones that negatively affect your physical and mental health.

Now, of course, there is only a correlation between smiling and a happy life—it certainly doesn't prove that smiling will make your marriage better or lengthen your life. Perhaps those who smiled most were just innately happier people or smiled more because life was already treating them well in college, predicting more good things to come. Studies such as these can't show what causes what. Waves are correlated with beaches, but do beaches cause waves or waves bring beaches?

But if one assumes that those who smile more will be happier, what happens to those who smile less? Shouldn't those who developed difficulty smiling as adults suffer more from depression, all other things being equal? Nature has done the experiment if one knows where to look. To probe for cause and effect, doctors studied what happened to patients who, because of facial nerve damage, were unable to move their faces normally. The facial nerve is commonly damaged in adult life by a condition known as Bell's palsy. There are three major parts of the facial nerve, so it is possible to lose the ability to frown but be able to smile, or vice versa. These researchers asked their patients to raise their eyebrows, squint, smile, and pucker their mouths to assess the extent of their facial disability. Their hypothesis was that the inability to smile would increase one's risk of depression. The results showed that a general impairment in moving one's face was not associated with depression. However, patients who specifically lacked the ability to smile were much more likely to become depressed, and their depression was more severe. There are several possible explanations. First, smiling occurs in social situations and helps facilitate positive emotions and relationships with others. Those individuals who find themselves unable to smile may experience more social isolation, leading to more depressive symptoms from loneliness. This could be a strong negative feedback loop. Second, smiling, by activation of the smile muscle, would initiate a feedback loop to the brain, activating our happy part of the brain, contributing to a more positive mood and more smiling. Those with impaired smiling would have the positive feedback interrupted and more consistent weight on the side of depression. I believe the second explanation is more important, but there is no evidence to help us decide.

Most of the time, the smile is a strongly positive signal. But our social relationships are so complex, and evolution has had such a long time to graft one thing on another, that sometimes a smile may have other meanings.

You can count on artists and writers to intuitively sense the nuances of human emotions and facial expressions. Long before science started to tackle the smile, Nathaniel Hawthorne wrote in *The Scarlet Letter* about a "haughty" smile, a "disdainful" smile, a "bitter" smile, a "mocking" smile, a "grave" smile, a "puzzled" smile, a "sad" smile, a "solemn" smile, and even a "sneering" smile. The list goes on and on. Our understanding of smiling has only recently caught up to the art of his description.

How could a smile mean so many different things? The answer is that it doesn't. A smile is fundamentally a positive signal. However, one facial expression can qualify another. Suppose you have just buried a relative, and a friend comes up to you at the funeral. You have a sad expression because you are sad, but you also add a little smile after the expression of sadness to let your friend know that you are going to be okay. That is Hawthorne's "sad" smile. Or perhaps you forgot to take out the garbage, which is one of your responsibilities. Your wife is angry with you, and she shows some anger in her brow. But she wants to let you know that all is not lost, so she adds a little smile after her frown to modulate her anger.

An unhappy person can smile, masking other emotions, such as fear or anxiety. Suppose you are about to get your blood drawn and you are a little bit afraid. But you want to reassure the phlebotomist that you are not going to move your arm, so you show a mouth smile in addition to the fear that is showing on your brow.

What if you had a friend who was depressed enough to have attempted suicide at one time? You ask her how she is doing. She is still depressed but doesn't want you to worry about her, so she smiles to try and mask her sadness. The smile can qualify or mask any other facial expression, either unconsciously or consciously. Many times a perfunctory smile is just a result of cultural customs that call for a smile on an initial greeting. Usually you can differentiate that smile from a true Duchenne smile by its absence of eye smiling.

Unfortunately, a smile can occasionally be devious. An evil mind can voluntarily trigger smiles. The smile can be much more deceptive than the frown. It is much easier to simulate a smile than a frown. If someone is about to do something unscrupulous to a colleague, he or she may be feeling some hostile emotions toward that individual. If they meet that individual unexpectedly, they may mask their true intentions by smiling, deceiving their unwitting associate. As Hamlet says just after he finds out that his uncle murdered his father:

O villain, villain, smiling, damned villain!
... That one may smile, and smile, and be a villain;
At least I am sure it may be so in Denmark.

IN THE SEVENTEENTH century, the philosopher René Descartes had a profound influence on Western thought. He firmly believed that human existence began with our thoughts. His famous statement "I think therefore I am" created sharp boundaries between the mind and the body and led future Western philosophers and scientists to stubbornly resist the idea that the mind's power extends far beyond its physical limits, far beyond the brain's traditional functions. Although physically we may have a three-pound masterpiece of invention resting on top of our necks, our minds and bodies are much more interconnected than it might appear. Since many of the connections are not made by nerves that we can see and feel, we have been slow to recognize just how inseparable our bodies and minds really are and how dependent our physical health is on our mental health. Eastern medicine has intuited for millennia that the brain and the body are intimately intertwined, intact, and inseparable. We are beginning to understand that what cannot be easily seen may be true nonetheless.

Buddhism's 2,500-year tradition of meditation has recognized the intricate web of the mind-body complex and how the state of mind has direct effects on overall health and well-being.

For example, in Tibetan medicine, two of the most important factors believed to affect a patient's recovery from illness are the mindsets of both the doctor and the patient.

How does meditation relate to smiling? Recently, neuroscientists have applied sophisticated neuroimaging tools such as PET scanning to examine the brain during the meditative state. They found that a meditating Tibetan monk shows high levels of activity in the left prefrontal cortex region of the brain. This happens to be the same area of the brain that is more active when we are happy. This monk's left prefrontal cortex lit up to a high level of "happiness" during his meditative state. But even when this monk was not meditating, his left prefrontal cortex showed unusually high activity. Tibetan Buddhist monks typically practice a type of meditation that involves the generation of an unconditional feeling of loving-kindness and compassion that pervades the whole mind. Traditionally, monks spend years learning how to meditate. During meditation they focus on compassionate thoughts initially for themselves; this is then broadened to friends, "neutral" people, enemies, and, finally, all sentient beings. One can conclude that the years Buddhist monks spend meditating allow them to control the part of the brain that sets happiness levels. It appears that it's possible to cultivate empathy and happiness through skill training, akin to the way we get better at music or sports through repeated practice. One can envision a less violent world where children practice the skills of empathy and compassion through meditation, accomplishing through an indirect method of what we may have more trouble teaching directly.

How does this ability of Tibetan monks relate to facial expressions? It turns out that the same area of the brain—the prefrontal cortex—is activated when we smile. By physically expressing a display of happiness, a smile, we activate an area of the brain that monks activate by compassion meditation. While at first glance this is unexpected, it drives home how interconnected with ourselves we really are. You can activate the same part of the brain by travelling along different roads, whether by meditating or by smiling.

Unfortunately, most of us cannot easily spend years meditating in a Buddhist monastery. But researchers have recently shown the power of meditation for others. They asked a simple and practical question: Can eight weeks of meditation training and practice in stressed-out Western biotech workers mimic the brain pattern that a monk creates after years of practice? Lo and behold, the activity of the left (happy) prefrontal cortex increased, and the workers reported feeling happier and more satisfied with their work. For those of us who have not yet learned to meditate, perhaps we should try smiling for 20 minutes a day.

CHAPTER 5

WRINKLER ABOVE THE EYE

"The world is a looking-glass, and gives back to every man the reflection of his own face. Frown at it, and it will in turn look sourly upon you; laugh at it and with it, and it is a jolly kind companion; and so let all young persons take their choice."
—William Makepeace Thackeray

WHY DO WE frown? At first glance, this may seem like an easy question to answer, but as soon as you study frowning in depth, you realize just how complex it can be. First, we frown for many different reasons. Most of the time we frown when we are communicating our emotions to others. We frown when we're worried, we're concerned, and we don't know what to do. But we also frown when we are frustrated or just struggling to understand something. If you are working on a hard math problem, you may frown without being aware of it. And we clearly frown when we are angry or sad. When my friend's father died, I first learned about it when I saw her face—her eyebrows were drawn together in such a way that I felt her sadness. A frown may pass over our brow in less than a second or it may persist for months or years.

Second, there are different types of frowns depending on what other muscles in our faces are activated at the same time. The meaning of your frown depends, in part, on how the other facial muscles are recruited to form a facial expression. If the inner part of your eyebrows point upward while frowning, you look sad (Figure 5.2); if they are drawn together and down while frowning, you look angry (Figure 5.1). And all of this activity happens so seamlessly, without a hiccup, day after day. Just as your voice carries your emotions as you speak, your facial muscles cooperate to give others an idea of your emotions and feelings. As we shall see again and again in this book, your frown speaks to you without your being aware of it.

The intensity of facial expressions usually correlates with the intensity of the emotion felt. If you are in a rage, your brow will most likely be tightly contracted—if you are only annoyed, a fleeting and subtle frown may pass over your brow.

The frown is an amazingly versatile and subtle form of expression. It is like an adjective that has so many nuances that it occupies a whole page of entries in the *Oxford English Dictionary* or a stage actor who can play roles written by William Shakespeare or Arthur Miller. If you videotape a conversation with a friend and replay it slowly, you will see that your frown muscles constantly communicate, along with your words, adding visual queries, expressions of puzzlement, and fleeting gestures of disapproval. Take one of your favorite tennis matches (I suggest Nadal vs. Djokovic) and slow it down to one-eighth speed—you will be surprised by how much the players' faces are moving. Their arms and legs are only part of the match.

The frown is naturally like a good director, controlling the movement of lighting and scenery, marking transitions, changing mood and feeling, giving tempo to our conversations. All of this activity that is happening around our eyebrows is not recognized in a conscious way. Most of it happens so quickly (in seconds) and so fleetingly that we do not remember it. However, in spite of the unconscious and involuntary nature of these emotional signals, our brains are taking it all in, assessing the meaning of the facial expressions of others, and responding in turn with our own facial expressions.

Charles Darwin was the first to note that the frown starts early in infancy. Observing his own children, he was able to deduce that a frown came over his child's brow whenever anything difficult presented itself. He described how, with his own infant, "little frowns...may be seen incessantly passing like shadows over its face" when something displeasing happened to him.

Darwin noted how his eight-week-old could easily express his annoyance at being fed not straight from the breast, but with cold milk. Clearly, at an early stage in human life, we acquire the ability to frown, suggesting how important this expression must be for our survival. Long before his baby cried, a little frown alerted the caregiver that babies prefer warm milk.

We all instinctively recognize the different ways in which people can express emotion. Body posture and movement are important; picture the slumped carriage of the dejected and despondent, or the triumphant bearing of the fans whose team just scored. And the human voice, with its dramatic range of timbre and tonality, can project the ebullience of joy as easily as the depths of despair. The inflection of our voices can tell us so much about a loved one—is the voice calm and soothing or does it reveal underlying anxiety or sadness? But it is easier to hide the emotions carried by your voice or body posture. You can decide to be silent if you don't want to let on how angry you are about what your husband just said to you, and we also have good voluntary control of the muscles that determine our posture. You don't have to clench your fist if you are angry—you can easily pretend that all is well by keeping your body relaxed. But it is much harder for most of us to hide our emotions from our faces. It all happens so quickly—different emotions display themselves on our faces in a second or less—before we are aware of what our faces are doing. Unless you have a lot of training, it will be difficult for you to hide the feelings that your face shows to others. The face thus assumes greater importance in your emotional interactions with others.

In addition, the face, with its complex and dynamic interwoven muscle skin layer, can convey a more complex range of our emotions than either the contortion of our bodies or the sound of our voices. For example, how do you show disgust with either your body or your voice? One might transmit irritation or annoyance with one's voice, but disgust? However, to recognize facial signals you must pay attention. Unlike words, which we continue to hear even if we don't want to, if we change the direction of our gaze, we may miss an important part of the conversation. In spite of these limitations, the face is still the most powerful and specific signal of emotion. And your brain thinks so as well. The area of our brain that helps us remember and distinguish between faces has evolved over countless generations to be much larger than the part that helps us decode emotions in speech because it is more important to understand the meaning of those faces around us.

THE MAIN MUSCLE involved in the facial expressions of sadness and anger is called the *corrugator supercilii*. The two Latin words that make up the name literally mean "the wrinkler above the eye." The corrugator muscle, the frown muscle, helps draw the eyebrows together to create a frown.

Frowning is a facial expression that usually represents negative emotional feelings. If our smiles tell others that all is good, our frowns do the reverse. The negativity may be mild, as in Darwin's baby's reacting to drinking cold milk, or it could be the extreme frown of sadness when one learns of the death of a parent. With fear, the entire brow is lifted, and the brows are often drawn together. In the frown of sadness, the inside corners of the brow are tilted up, and the upper eyelids are arched up. Each of these frowns carries a distinct meaning, and the intensity of the frown alerts us to the intensity of the emotion.

The frown muscle is not the only facial muscle activated in the expression of sadness, fear, or anger. For example, in anger the eyelids are tensed and the teeth may be bared (Figure 5.1). Here we see a face of extreme anger during a soccer match.

Figure 5.1   Angry man

In sadness, the lower eyelid may be raised while the corners of the mouth are drawn down. But just as the smile muscle helps pull the corners of our mouths up and out, and is most associated with smiling and happiness, so the muscle in the eyebrow remains the strongest means of expressing anger or sadness. These two muscles—the frown and smile muscles—represent the yin and yang of facial expressions.

I often look to the arts to help understand aspects of humanity that are not so easily decipherable with the scientific tools at hand. Artists have for most of human history been the most astute observers, recorders, and implicit analysts of the link among expression, emotion, and state of mind, from the most extreme states of joy and anguish to the subtlest shifts of mood. One of the sculptural wonders of the ancient world, the *Laocoön*, is perhaps the most iconic portrayal of the frown muscle. The Greek statue *Laocoön and His Sons* was carved in marble on the island of Rhodes in the first century BCE. Sometime after that, *Laocoön* disappeared into history, its renown kept alive by the writings of the ancient Roman historian Pliny, who basically said it was the best piece of artwork ever made. And this is in comparison to all the art made by the ancient Greeks! What made *Laocoön* so special?

In the classical story, Laocoön was a Trojan priest who had warned against allowing the gigantic wooden horse presented by the Greeks to be brought into the city of Troy and hurled his spear into the horse's flank. The Roman poet Virgil describes how the gods punished him by sending a pair of giant sea serpents to strangle him and his sons.

The central figure is so lifelike, with Laocoön's taut and heroic muscles projecting emotion in their final, fatal struggle. And the entire sculpture is beautifully sculpted. But what is really so remarkable is the profound sense of agony, defeat, and sadness seen in Laocoön's face. His eyebrows are drawn together and upward as his head tilts with suffering. His eyebrows are pure sadness, as Laocoön realizes he will lose this battle. His frown has the intensity one sees on the face of someone who has just learned of their child's death—in this case, Laocoön knows that he and his sons are not long for this world. Notice how his face shows no sense of a fight, no sense of anger at his enemy, only a profound sense of loss. His mouth is softly opened, not tensed as a warrior charging into battle, nor grimaced as one might be if in severe physical pain or if angry. Here Laocoön suffers, but he suffers most from heart-wrenching emotional pain.

Figure 5.2   Laocoon, 20 BCE

Figure 5.3   Moses by Michelangelo, 1515

A team including Michelangelo, who helped identify the statue, rediscovered *Laocoön* early in the sixteenth century. The pathos of Laocoön's face deeply moved Michelangelo, and it shows in the wrathful face of his sculpture of Moses (Figure 5.3).

Here is Moses holding the stone tablets bearing the Ten Commandments that he has just brought back from Mount Sinai. He has led the Jews on their arduous journey out of Egypt but finds his people again worshipping the golden calf—the false idol they had made. Moses's anger and disapproval show clearly in his knitted, furrowed, and muscular brow. You can feel the steely resolve in his face. One gets the distinct impression that Moses has spent a lifetime lifting heavy emotional weights with his eyebrow muscles. His frown is palpable and powerful as it defies the prison of stone. We can read Moses's feelings as we look at this icon.

This sculpture is so emotive that even Freud, who was not generally interested in art, tried to psychoanalyze it. Freud thought that Michelangelo was trying to show how Moses was actively restraining himself from rising up with the anger he felt after he saw his people dancing around the golden calf.

THE FACT THAT the frown's first real flourish in art since the ancient Greeks takes place in the Renaissance is indicative of the period's renewed interest in empathy and humanism. You don't see too much emotion on the faces of Madonnas or kings and queens from the Middle Ages. Then the Renaissance began, and artists grew interested again in all the extremes of human emotion. Faces became alive again. It must be more than just a coincidence that some of the world's greatest artists, artists whose reputation has survived the test of time, have paid such close attention to facial expressions, in particular the frown (or, in Leonardo's case, the smile). These artists recognized, before many others, how powerfully our brows could show our innermost thoughts and feelings.

The tension and position of frown versus smile groups will help show others what you are feeling inside. That is common sense to most of us. But the relative contractions of each muscle will not only tell others your emotional state—they will inform you, the wearer of the expression, what you are feeling. And not only do these muscles silently speak to you—they help to create the state of your conscious mind. We shall see many examples of how the face you make influences your decisions and preferences. Your face helps you to both optimally sense and express your emotions, and the balance between the activity of these two muscles helps determine how you feel about the world outside and inside you.

CHAPTER 6

COMMUNICATION FROM THE UNCONSCIOUS

A WINDOW INTO FEELINGS

"Grief is the agony of an instant, the indulgence of grief the blunder of a lifetime."

—Benjamin Disraeli

I FIRST MET Sharon ten years ago. Then 42 years old, she was frustrated by the seemingly inexorable weight gain around her midsection. In losing the fine figure of her youth, she had lost much of her self-esteem. Her harshest critic was herself. She no longer felt attractive, and this was impairing her sexual life. Her husband tried to convince her otherwise but to no avail. Sharon came to see me about improving her figure with liposuction. After I explained to her that we performed the entire procedure under local anesthesia, Sharon told me that local anesthesia usually didn't work for her at the dentist. Whenever patients tell me that local anesthesia doesn't work for them, three thoughts enter my mind: maybe the doctor didn't quite hit the right spot, maybe the patient really is more sensitive to pain, or maybe the memory of one bad experience made any subsequent discomfort all the more disturbing.

On the day of the surgery, Sharon reminded me again that she didn't respond to anesthesia. I assured her that with the right amount, everything would be fine. As I do with most patients, I gave Sharon Valium to help her relax while she was prepped for surgery.

An hour later, after her husband kissed her goodbye and left the surgical suite, it struck me how anxious Sharon was. The Valium hadn't done much. I would need to be extra careful to make sure that her experience with liposuction was nothing like her memory of dentistry.

Standing with her in front of a mirror as we decided together on which areas of fat to treat, I knew she was going to need some special attention to get her through the surgery comfortably. After we numbed her abdomen, I made a tiny incision in Sharon's abdomen. Then I inserted a small hollow metal tube into her abdomen and began liposuction. I looked at Sharon's face—she was relaxed and sleeping like a baby (the Valium had finally kicked in). Everything went well for about 15 minutes until I started operating over her ribs; then I noticed her brow begin to furrow. The ribs are a more sensitive area. She was still asleep. I returned my instrument to her abdominal area, and her eyebrows became more relaxed. But when I started operating over her ribs again, her corrugator muscle began contracting again. My own anxiety went up a notch. I was performing liposuction on Sharon using local anesthesia, and the last thing I wanted was for her to experience even the slightest discomfort.

It is well documented that even under general anesthesia, a few patients will remember the pain when the surgeon began the incision—sometimes they are under just deep enough to lose all voluntary control of their muscles but not deep enough to be unable to feel some pain. (One of my patients described to me how she developed post-traumatic stress disorder from delivering her first child. She vividly remembers feeling powerless as her doctor began the emergency C-section—she still felt all the pain and was unable to tell him.)

Pain. Even looking at the word can cause one to wince. When we see it in others, it triggers those remarkable neurons called mirror neurons that make us empathetic and allow us to feel the suffering of a fellow human being. But local anesthesia isn't perfect. The only way to know if the skin is numb is to test it. Sometimes an area looks quite numb, but as you cut tissue, you can encounter some surprises. Everything can be numb except for one spot! A little more local anesthesia corrects the problem, but pain is a genie that's hard to put back into the bottle once it has been released. The patient will always remember the painful part of the procedure and forget the rest.

Our fears and anxiety frequently alter our experience. Our brains can easily forget many an important fact, like the name of your friendly coworker on a Monday morning before coffee. But try forgetting a really scary experience. The emotions we feel during such moments stamp our memories so strongly into our minds that it is as if our recollection has been carved into stone. I suspect that when we relive those terrifying moments in our minds, our muscles of facial expression assume, in part, the state they had when we actually lived through the experience. Our faces are part and parcel of the emotion and thus would also be part of the memory.

I once operated to remove a skin cancer from the forehead of a woman who, years before, had been involved in a bad accident that sent her into the windshield. She emerged, dazed and bleeding, from the car. In the emergency room, they removed dozens of minute pieces of glass from her forehead. Unfortunately, she saw her bloodied forehead in the metallic reflection from a surgical lamp, and that traumatic image stayed with her. Many years later, when she saw the bloody wound that I had created in removing a skin cancer from the same area, her mind travelled back to the time of the car accident. She now vividly recalled the Puma sneakers that one of the assistants had been wearing as they sewed her up and smelled again the odor of an active emergency room. Only later did she explain to me why she had gotten so anxious with our surgery. All those old memories came flooding back, including the dreaded Puma sneakers.

One of the holy grails of modern neuroscience is the ability to selectively remove painful and stressful memories. Think of all the soldiers of war who survive the war but lose their way in life. Their readjustment to civilian life would be so much easier if a few traumatic memories could be erased.

The brain's remarkable ability to remember fear and danger is due in part to the amygdala, an almond-shaped part of our midbrain that is important in regulating our emotions, especially the negative ones. It does not want you to forget things that should be feared. Hence the difficulty in treating post-traumatic stress disorder.

The amygdala has its reasons. If you forget about the first time that a bear chases you away from her cubs, you may not live to remember the second time you get too close to baby bears. Fearful memories are meant to protect us from further harm. But sometimes they just do their job too well. They make us afraid of things we no longer have reason to fear, forcing us to live in the past.

In monkeys the amygdala is activated by fear; if a monkey's amygdala is removed, it is unable to learn to avoid painful shocks. In people the amygdala is crucial in orchestrating our perception of, and response to, emotions. It's a sort of brain within the brain that is crucial for emotions, a command and control center—a hub that sends out connections to many parts of the brain to help coordinate what happens when we see that bear in the backyard. It turns out that the amygdala can help explain the theories of William James and Freud.

When you hear a gunshot or see a bear running toward you, information is quickly transmitted to the thalamus (another deep part of the brain) and then directly to the amygdala. This is a fast and unconscious pathway that helps get you out of the way of danger as quickly as possible. From the amygdala, connections go to the hypothalamus, the part of the brain that helps mediate the unconscious aspects of emotion, such as sweating, blood pressure, and heart rate. This is why your heart starts thumping in your chest after you hear a gunshot. Information about what the hypothalamus is doing is then sent to your cortex, and that is when you consciously feel the emotion, consciously feel scared. This pathway takes more time than the unconscious pathway. When the brilliant psychologist William James spoke of your being consciously aware of being afraid only after your muscles and body experience the fear, this is what he meant. And when Freud spoke of your unconscious emotion influencing your conscious decision making, this probably represents the emotional signals from the amygdala that eventually reach your cortex, your consciousness, telling you what to do.

The amygdala helps decide the valence, positive or negative, of an emotion. In addition, it grades the intensity of the emotion. And it responds to fearful or angry facial expressions more than to happy ones. In this way it can help translate what we see on the face into emotional feelings.

BACK TO SHARON on the operating table. She was still asleep but would not remain so for long if the operation started to hurt. I stopped, injected more local anesthesia around her ribs, and switched to a small diameter cannula. Smaller instruments are less painful. This would slow the procedure down a bit, but it would also decrease the possibility that Sharon would feel any pain. I began again to remove fat while keeping a close watch on her eyebrows. They had relaxed, indicating that she was feeling fine. Her unconscious spoke to me as her forehead remained calm, and she slept through the rest of the operation.

Sharon taught me to look at two things during surgery: the operating field and the patient's brow. Whoever said that the eyes are the window to the soul almost had it right. Actually it's the muscles around the eyes and between the brows that provide a sensitive measure of our feelings. These muscles provide a visible barometer of pain. First the eyebrows draw downward and together. At the same time, the muscle around the orbit of the eye, the orbicularis oculi, tightens and leads to a tensing of the eyelids.

For the sake of my patients' comfort and my own peace of mind, I watch for the first hint of a contraction of the corrugator muscle, the beginnings of a frown, rather than wait to hear the proverbial "OW!" Long before the pain becomes severe enough to reach consciousness and cause a patient to speak, it reaches deeper and evolutionarily older brain pathways that activate the facial nerve and tell the corrugator to contract. As soon as I see the corrugator twitch and the muscles around the eyes move in the wrong direction, I stop cutting and reach for the local anesthetic. I call this the corrugator sign, and I always heed its advice, knowing that it comes straight and true from the source.

YOU DEFINITELY DO not need your conscious brain for the corrugators to play their roles. Many a sleeping patient's corrugator has alerted me to the first hint of discomfort and enabled me to stop before the patient became consciously aware of it. That marvelous muscle, the corrugator, makes it possible to complete a procedure without ever interrupting the patient's peaceful rest.

I have been fortunate to learn to operate while patients are breathing on their own, still able to communicate with me, whether by their frown muscles while sleeping or by words and expressions if awake. But most surgeons are trained in the operating room and have anesthesiologists to administer the general anesthesia. Although physicians often use the euphemism of putting you to sleep for general anesthesia, they are not one and the same. If you are asleep and I pinch you, you will tell me pretty quickly to stop that. If you are under general anesthesia and I do the same, you do not respond at all. If your patient is unconscious with a breathing tube in place, there is no need to pay attention to their facial expression as the facial muscles are paralyzed by the general anesthesia. But my patients will move their faces during surgery, and that is hard to ignore.

I am privy to my patients' emotions during every surgery that I perform. Sometimes my eyes are just a foot away from my patients as I cut and sew. When I see a wince or grimace or frown, magnified by a surgical loop, it really registers in my brain. Those muscles of displeasure contracting on my patients' faces powerfully alert me to their suffering, making me feel their suffering and change the course of surgery before I hear any words.

It is a quirk of history that dermatologic surgery evolved from a medical specialty, dermatology, and therefore, the specialty evolved outside of the hospital-based operating suite. The culture of the dermatologic surgeon differs from that of the general surgeon the way German cuisine differs from Italian. One would never confuse a meal in Cologne with one in Rome, but you can eat well in both cities. Dermatologic surgeons had to develop the art of local anesthesia to allow them to operate on larger areas, whether to remove large skin cancers or fat. They did not have the option of operating on patients who had been rendered unconscious by general anesthesia.

Sometimes difficulties can lead to great advances. In the 1980s, an enterprising dermatologic surgeon named Jeffrey Klein was trying to figure out how to operate on a large part of a patient's body without general anesthesia. He discovered that one could dilute local anesthesia ten-fold and have it still provide good anesthesia for the removal of body fat by liposuction. He pioneered the use of diluted local anesthesia, known as tumescent anesthesia (it means to swell in Latin, based on how the skin and fat swell after the anesthesia is injected), which has allowed him and other dermatologic surgeons to safely operate on much larger areas without the need for general anesthesia. The great advantage of local anesthesia is that it is safe compared with general anesthesia, which always carries the risk that the patient may never wake up or may develop a deadly blood clot from prolonged immobility. The safety comes with a price, however; you must learn how to alleviate patients' anxiety and prevent their pain. Since all of my patients are breathing on their own, I have learned to observe their faces so that they can talk to me without words.

THE UNCONSCIOUS BRAIN is always around us, speaking through faces, if we only listen. I tried waking my 16-year-old daughter from her deep slumber one morning. She had stayed up late the night before, so I expected her to be tired. But I didn't expect what happened when I opened the door to her room and turned on the overhead light. As she semiconsciously raised her head, a not so subtle frown arose rapidly between her eyebrows. She had not even opened her eyes or truly emerged from sleep. But her corrugator muscle already knew what her conscious brain was not yet aware of: the light I had turned on was an unpleasant surprise seen by her retina through her closed, sleepy eyelids, and I had disturbed her restful sleep. Her unconscious brain registered her discomfort at the sudden bright light and spoke to me through her frown. And I instantly understood what she was trying to say. She was effectively communicating with me with her eyebrows. I am sure that at that instant she felt a twinge of displeasure pass through her as her eyebrows told her brain that something unpleasant was happening.

ONE DAY AS I was riding my bicycle in the bright sunshine, I failed to see a large hole in the middle of the road. The wheel fit the hole nicely and stayed put—but I kept on moving. Seconds, and a couple of broken ribs later, I lay screaming in agony on the pavement. I hadn't made a conscious decision to scream. My unconscious mind had taken over, reacting to the pain and the shock of uncertainty. My face contorted, and my vocal cords let out the most unambiguous sound—a scream of pain. I frowned as part of an involuntary signal directed by my unconscious engine. I was hardwired to scream and screw up my face to express what my body was feeling.

The next day I looked at myself in the mirror. I did not even recognize my body. All the muscles that usually provided the framework for standing erect were rebelling in pain. My torso now had an absurd twist, along with a newfound pot belly from a state of total abdominal muscle relaxation. The work these muscles normally performed was hidden from view until an injury revealed their contribution. My ribs and muscles had sent signals to my brain declaring their injury. In return, my brain had told them to stop contracting, thus reducing their pain. The unconscious way in which sensory information feeds back to our brain about the position, tone, and state of our muscles and joints, continually readjusting our bodies, is known as proprioception, literally "self-perception." The entire process relies on myriad sensory receptors in the muscles called proprioceptors. As Oliver Sacks says about owning and operating our physical selves in *The Man Who Mistook His Wife for a Hat and Other Clinical Tales*, "It is so automatic, so familiar, we never give it a thought."

So if we have all these pathways for the brain to track even the smallest changes in our body position and muscle health, isn't it more than likely that there is an equivalent pathway for our emotional state? A temperature gauge for our emotions must exist, deep in our brains, gathering information from our muscles, in this case the ones that are intimately involved in the generation of our emotions, the muscles of facial expression. Therefore, an efficient unconscious pathway exists to relay, in real time, our emotional state to our brain.

Most of the time the changes in our emotional state remain at the unconscious level because they are too small to filter up to the conscious level, too small to demand our attention. Our conscious feelings represent only a part of the emotional pathway; the rest of the time our bodies are experiencing emotions, but we are not consciously aware of them. Sometimes something big happens to us, something that our brain attaches a lot of emotion to, and then we become aware of our need to act and make a decision.

As I reflected on the link between emotion and facial expressions, I began to speculate about a parallel form of proprioception that I call emotional proprioception. It dawned on me that silent feedback from the facial muscles about their tension or state of contraction might also help guide our brains to feel emotions. Increased tension of the frown muscles might tell our brains that something unpleasant is happening. Perhaps every time you frown, however briefly, you are sending an impulse to your brain that says, "Get me out of here. I'm not happy." Conversely, if you smile, you send impulses back to say that all is well. One of the simpler ways for your brain to be aware of your emotions is to monitor the contraction of the various muscles in your face. Imagine that your brain is keeping track of how many times a day you smile, laugh, and frown and how strong those expressions are. Your brain would also be aware of whether you had frowns of sadness or anger, or polite social smiles versus smiles of true enjoyment. At the end of the day, your brain could add up the positive expressions and subtract the negative ones, giving your mind a kind of scorecard for what had transpired and what your overall state of mind was.

What if we could change the feedback that the brain is receiving from the facial muscles? Would that affect your emotional state and then your mood? If your brain really keeps score, with frowning on one side and smiling on the other, could you alter how the brain views the world around you? Could you wear rose-colored glasses by decreasing negative facial signals back to the brain? Or by sending more positive signals? I thought more about using this approach to treat patients clinically. Could I alter my patients' mood and make them happier simply by changing facial expressions?

CHAPTER 7

DARWIN AND FACIAL FEEDBACK

"If we fancy some strong emotion, and then try to abstract from our consciousness of it all the feelings of its bodily symptoms, we find we have nothing left behind."

—William James

WE HAVE SEEN how our faces give information to others about our thoughts, desires, and feelings. But does your face speak to you? And does facial muscle movement change our mood? There are actually much data to show that voluntary facial manipulation can change how one feels.

If changing your face can change your emotions and moods, then one might expect that actors can give us some insight into this process. For example, do they suffer after acting the parts of deranged characters?

The Academy Award–winning 1947 film *A Double Life* revolves around the relationship between emotion and facial expression. The central character, portrayed by Ronald Colman, plays the part of a famous actor. When the movie opens, the Colman character is a romantic leading man who is equally light-hearted when he is off as on stage. Asked to make his next starring role that of Othello, the Colman character initially resists taking the part. He had played Othello some years before, and his marriage broke up when his own emotional state came to mirror that of the character. Against his better judgment, he is persuaded to play the role again.

Night after night, Colman's character looks enraged, unhappy, and angst-filled onstage, as he relives *Othello*. In every scene, we see his face contorted, his brow furrowed, as he enacts the tragedy of the Moorish general who murders his innocent wife in a jealous rage. As the movie progresses, Colman's character becomes more and more deranged. We see him slowly lose his ability to leave behind the personality of Othello when he exits the theater each night. He turns sullen and suffers fleeting periods of irrationality followed by pro-longed amnesiac lapses. His face begins to replicate Othello's pained and demonic expressions, eventually morphing the man into a modern-day version of the character who jealously murders the woman he loves.

The movie leaves no doubt of its central thesis: that adopting murderous expressions onstage changed the Colman character as a person, as well as the inner workings of his mind, which transformed him into a murderer. This makes for an entertaining movie, but one wonders how relevant the story is. Does acting angry create angry feelings? When you act sad, do you actually become sadder in real life?

Andrew Ellmore, a New York psychologist, has described a similar situation in his treatment of a soap opera actor who daily acted the part of a depressed, tearful wife whose husband continually cheats on her. When the depression carried over into the actor's own life, Dr. Ellmore asked the screenwriters to rewrite her character so that her husband treats her better. Remarkably, this resulted in lifting the woman's true depression.

What does it mean to really enter the persona of another? If you are really good at role playing, you pick up on the thoughts, feelings, habits, and very essence of the character you are trying to re-create, and you mimic their behavior so well that we call you a great actor. As far back as the eighteenth century, the great German dramatist Gotthold Ephraim Lessing suggested that when "the actor properly imitates all the external signs... and all the bodily... expressions of a particular [inner] state," then he will re-create in his own being all the emotions, thoughts, and feelings of the acted part.

The modern method actor would wholeheartedly agree. To portray someone suffering bereavement, the method actor will re-create the appropriate facial expressions to activate memories that correspond to the experience of emotional loss. The feelings triggered in this way deepen the facial expression and make the portrayal of a character even more realistic. But sometimes an actor can play a role so well that she still feels the emotions when she is finished acting.

It's hard to imagine how it wouldn't affect the real you if, with great fidelity, you repeatedly assumed the face and feelings of someone very sad. It's not unusual to hear of an actor who so faithfully relives the part of a depressed, demonized character that once the role playing is done, it takes a while for them to recover from the effect it had on them.

IN THE FIRST half of the 1800s, in *Essays on the Anatomy and Philosophy of Expression*, Charles Bell provided the first hint of the facial feedback hypothesis when he wrote that perhaps "by the actions and expressions of the body betraying the passions of the heart we may be startled and forewarned, as it were, by the reflection of ourselves, and at the same time learn to control our passions by restraining the expression of them."

Darwin picked up where Bell left off when he described "the intimate relation which exists between almost all the emotions and their outward manifestation and partly from the direct influence of exertion on the heart, and consequently on the brain."

William James, a Harvard psychologist, was a visionary when he elaborated on his facial feedback theory of emotion in his landmark 1890 work, *Principles of Psychology*. James suggested that our muscles contribute to our emotions. If, for example, we tense our thighs and clench our fists as we prepare to fight, we will feel angrier. He theorized that changes in the muscles are occurring all the time to suit the emotions of the moment even if we are consciously unaware of them. James said, "Smooth the brow, brighten the eye," stand up straight, "and speak in major key, pass the genial compliment, and your heart must be frigid indeed if it does not gradually thaw!"

But James's theories fell out of favor until the 1960s, when Silvan Tomkins, a charismatic psychologist, took James's proposals and assigned a special role to the face. He suggested that sensations provided by emotional expressions of the face are the source of the different emotional feelings, distinguishing happiness from sadness, anger from fear. He stressed the concept of feedback from facial muscles to the brain in the experience of emotion and argued that specific categories of emotion evolved for certain functional, adaptive reasons. He explained that "the face expresses affect both to others, and to the self, via feedback, which is more rapid and complex than any stimulation of which the slower moving visceral organs (heart, liver, adrenal, kidney) are capable." Tomkins carefully described emotional categories and their corresponding facial expressions. He argued that the emotional system is the primary motivator for a wide range of human behavior.

Tomkins changed the history of psychology by convincing young researchers to get the kind of data that he thought would stimulate more research into the roles the face played in emotions. If these researchers could show that all humans made the same facial expressions—and that they meant the same thing in any part of the world—then others would join the research. He also knew that science lives and breathes on replication—without it no discovery has lasting importance. Not only did he impart his ideas and enthusiasm for research on facial expressions to Paul Ekman; he also convinced Carroll Izard to do the same experiment to determine the universality of facial expressions across cultural and racial divides. But he discreetly avoided telling either researcher that they had company—he wanted independent replication of the results, knowing full well that this would more powerfully change the scientific paradigm. They were both more than a little surprised and resentful to learn that they were not alone in their findings of universality of facial expressions, but in the end, Tomkins helped them both. And Tomkins was right—their research helped convince a generation of psychologists to create a new field studying emotion and facial expressions.

To realize how contrary to the prevailing dogma Tomkins's ideas were at the time, it is helpful to hear Paul Ekman's firsthand account:

> I began the project [to study the universality of facial expressions] believing that expression and gesture were socially learned and culturally variable, and so did the initial group of people I asked for advice. [He asked the leading anthropologists of the time, like Margaret Mead.] I recalled that Charles Darwin had made the opposite claim, but I was so convinced that he was wrong that I didn't bother to read his book. (You can't buy this kind of honesty anywhere. Have you ever read a scientist admitting how completely wrong he was?)

Ekman continues: "The...stroke of luck was meeting Silvan Tomkins. He had just written two books about emotion in which he claimed that facial expressions were innate and universal to our species, but he had no evidence to back up his claims....I was very impressed with the depth and breadth of Silvan's thinking, but I thought he was probably wrong in his belief, like Darwin's, that expressions were innate and therefore universal." Ekman was happy that his experiments would help settle a burning question at the time—whether Stone Age man could make and understand the same expressions on his face as a

DARWIN AND FACIAL FEEDBACK

modern-day college student. The thinking at the time was very polarized, with most of the anthropologists believing that facial expressions vary according to culture and learning. Heredity was assuming a smaller role in human behavior for scientists in the 1960s. It was more popular then to believe that almost every part of human behavior was driven by social learning.

Ekman goes on to say that, "There was a real argument between famous scientists,...and I, at age thirty, had the chance...to try to settle it once and for all: Are expressions universal, or are they, like language, specific to each culture? Irresistible!"

Fortunately for us, Ekman was not only up to the challenge, but listened to his own data rather than to the strongly held opinions of some of the more famous anthropologists at the time.

Tomkins turned out to be right about the face being the most important visual that humans pay attention to. Eric Kandel, the Nobel Prize–winning neuroscientist, writes: "Each face is unique; it is as much the visual signature of an individual human being as a fingerprint is. Yet while most people are unable to recognize and remember the whorls of a magnified fingerprint, each of us without conscious effort can recognize and remember hundreds, even thousands of faces."

Kandel goes on to explain how the human brain has a special way of perceiving faces. Unlike the way the brain processes other visual images, faces are recognized in the brain using a template to fit them into, an oval with two dots for the eyes, a vertical line between the dots for the nose, and a horizontal line below for the mouth. In this way you can quickly recognize and remember the face of your fellow human. There are also regions of the brain where almost every neuron responds only to a face. These specialized regions contain a face-recognition system that is able to recognize a face from any angle—quite a remarkable feat. In addition, this system does not depend on learning to be functional. And the brain assigns more processing power to faces than to the perception and processing of any other figural image.

The importance of face recognition for humans develops early. Infants are more likely to look at a face than at any other object. And as any mother will tell you, babies like to imitate our facial expressions. If you smile at your infant, she will more than likely smile back. At three months, infants begin to distinguish among different faces, an important development for their attachment to their parents. Recognition and interpretation of faces has clearly been important for the development and survival of humans.

How DOES ONE prove that changing your facial expression affects your emotions? In the early 1970s, researchers began performing experiments which suggested that adopting a particular facial pattern of emotion (e.g., fear, anger, disgust, sadness, happiness) induces the feeling of the particular emotion, even in the absence of any causal event. For example, if you smile and laugh more when watching a cartoon, you actually rate the cartoon as funnier (TV producers apparently discovered the same result independently when they introduced canned laugh tracks in the 1950s). The experimental studies became more sophisticated over time. Most of the work suggested that increasing smiling muscle activity led to a more positive evaluation of whatever was in front of one, whether it was a movie, a cartoon, a story, or an imagined event. Conversely, smiling less or frowning more cast a dark shadow on how you felt about what you saw or thought about. Still, there were many criticisms that could be made of some of the work. Were the subjects' evaluations of their own emotions affected by their conscious knowledge of the experimenters' aims?

To try and eliminate any role that the conscious mind might have played in some of the earlier experiments on emotions, researchers designed ever more ingenious experiments. They asked subjects to hold a pen either with their teeth (thus facilitating smiling by contracting the zygomaticus muscle) or in their lips (inhibiting the smile) while they rated the funniness of cartoons. Try it. You really have to smile if you hold a pen between your teeth, and you are absolutely prevented from doing so if the pen is between your lips.

They provided a good cover story for their experiment so that the students had no idea what the real purpose was. The subjects were told that the purpose of the study was to investigate the ability of handicapped persons to perform different tasks with different parts of the body. The authors found that participants holding the pen with their teeth (making them smile) felt more amused and rated the cartoons funnier than those who were prevented from smiling. They concluded that people's own perception of the meaning of the face they make is not necessary to influence the experience of emotion. Smiling, even if you are not aware of why you are doing it, makes the world look and feel rosier. This certainly fits with the concept of unconscious emotion influencing decision making.

This work has been followed up by studies that show a good correlation between the intensity of the smile and the internal emotional effect it produces. The next experiment sounds more absurd but really gave important results. To test the facial feedback hypothesis for the frown, golf tees were attached to both sides of the volunteer subjects' foreheads. They were asked to try and move the tees closer together. The only way to accomplish this is by contracting your corrugator muscles, thus simulating a frown. They then showed their volunteers photographs with emotional content. When the tees were closer together (frown expression), subjects rated unpleasant photographs more negatively. So the simple act of moving your forehead actually influences how you respond emotionally to an image and how you make a decision. This experiment shows that, irrespective of why you are frowning, it can cast a blue tint on your evaluation of the world around you. All of these experiments test your evaluation of the external world, but a recurring theme of this book is that frowning will cast a blue tint on your evaluation of your internal world, including your body, brain, and mind. And that includes your state of mind.

As you can see, psychologists and neuroscientists have had to be highly inventive in order to investigate human behavior. They need to hide their motives from their subjects so that the experimenters' bias is unknown to the people they are testing. When I worked as a molecular biologist cloning recombinant growth factors into viruses, there was less confusion about my results. I either isolated the right clone or I didn't. Viruses do not know about placebos or bias. And experiments in molecular biology are usually a lot easier and less expensive to repeat.

Human emotions are more transient, more nebulous, more evasive, and harder to quantify.

One group of researchers realized that the pronunciation of certain vowels causes the contraction of unique sets of facial muscles. For example, the inclusion of the German vowel *u* in a word will prevent its speaker from contracting the zygomaticus muscle, or smiling. In addition, pronunciation of the German *u* will help create a frown. They asked each native German speaker to read aloud two stories. One story contained many words (such as Gunter) that contained the vowel *u*; the other story contained no *u* words. Each story was written to be equivalent in terms of emotional tone and semantic content. After reading the stories aloud, subjects were asked to compare the stories in terms of quality of the prose, suitability for children, resemblance to a fairy tale, and, most importantly, which of the two was more pleasant and which the subject liked better. The subjects liked the no-*u* stories significantly better than the *u* stories, but they found no differences between the two stories in any of the other parameters. The authors concluded that muscular movements of the face are sufficient to affect how much we like something, sufficient to affect our emotions. Taking this to the next level, we would conclude that we probably do think and feel differently depending on what language we are speaking at the moment. Movements of the mouth necessitated by language should influence who we really are and might influence why the people in a country speaking one language behave differently than their neighbors across the border.

Now let us take a real-world experiment—the supermarket checkout tabloids. Subjects were asked to rate the fame of celebrities in the magazines we all look at while waiting in line. Lo and behold, volunteers who were asked to simultaneously furrow their brows reported the same celebrities to be less famous. Frowning appears to negatively influence how we evaluate many things, including our appraisal of our favorite movie star.

JANE WAS SITTING across from me in the airport, working away on her laptop, as we both waited for our flight to Burlington, Vermont. As she looked down at her computer, her face became more and more animated, her frown muscles working feverishly. But the moment they called our flight, her frown instantly vanished. My curiosity piqued, I asked her what she was working on. I explained that I was doing research on frowning, and that I could not help but notice that she had a powerful one. She said she had been concentrating on a letter to her associates back home in New Zealand. She was focusing so intensely, struggling to find the right words, that she frowned vigorously. She then proceeded to relate her own experience with how one's face affects one's mood.

The previous year she had been lucky enough to have the opportunity to spend several weeks in Paris, in glorious springtime, on a work assignment. Jane had been looking forward to this assignment—to be required to work in Paris in May is a requirement that many of us wouldn't mind. She was delighted by Paris, but not by all the unwanted and unexpected attention she received from the young Frenchmen. She couldn't go anywhere without having to fend off very persistent admirers who knew by her dress that she was not French. Jane was a tall, attractive young woman with curly reddish hair who found herself unable to walk down the street and enjoy the Parisian spring all by herself. She was used to the social customs of New Zealand, where a woman sitting alone would be left alone unless she invited company. Her first few days had been quite a struggle until she noticed that many of the young, attractive native Parisian women had a kind of permanent sneer on their faces. They seemed to be left alone, so Jane decided to adopt their expression of slight disgust. And it worked! The men who used to harass her now left her alone. But a week later, after purposefully keeping an expression of disgust on her face, beautiful Paris no longer seemed beautiful to her, and she at first wondered, and then concluded, that her imposed facial expression was diminishing her enjoyment of springtime in Paris. What amazed me was how Jane, a dedicated economist, without any knowledge or training in psychology, had deduced the facial feedback hypothesis all by herself. By the time I spoke to her, she viewed it not as a theory, but as something very real, something that fixed one problem but created another.

WE HAVE SEEN the interrelationships between the face and the emotions. The category of emotions is not at all simple to define but is important for our understanding of how facial expressions are woven into the complex fabric of human behavior. To understand the next set of studies, it will be helpful to learn more about emotions, how they evolved, how they are generated within us, and their crucial adaptive role for our survival. Let us start by asking a few questions.

What are emotions? Why do we have them? Do animals have them? At first glance, we may think we have a pretty good answer to these questions, but it behooves us to visit the subject with fresh eyes.

Emotions have been defined in many different ways by philosophers and psychologists over the ages. But instead of reviewing and assessing the various theories that have been put forth in the absence of any real data, let us view emotions through a window based on recent research by leading neuroscientists. Although the themes presented here are accepted by many, the study of emotion remains a field that contains a diversity of opinion.

The systems in our brains that help generate emotional behavior have evolved over long timelines, honed over countless generations and species. All organisms have to fill certain needs to survive in the world. At a minimum, they must find food for themselves and their kin, maintain the integrity of their tissues by providing enough oxygen and nutrients, and find sexual partners and pass their genes on to the next generation. They also have to find shelter from hostile environments and predators.

In addition to all the requirements for survival in the outside world, organisms have to maintain an ideal internal world in order to keep their muscles, brain, heart, lungs, and other organs working efficiently. The maintenance of the internal state, or homeostasis (from Greek *homoios*, similar, and *stasis*, standing still), requires constant monitoring along with a myriad of interconnected feedback loops. Without internal maintenance, the organism cannot survive. If your blood sugar were not tightly regulated by insulin secreted from your pancreas and a healthy drive to eat when your blood sugar fell too low, you would collapse into a coma fairly quickly. Something as simple as getting up from a chair requires coordination of your heart and circulatory system to maintain your blood pressure; if your body is faulty at this, you might faint when standing up as the blood pools in your legs and your blood pressure drops. And if you didn't get thirsty, the concentrations of sodium and potassium ions in your blood would waver too far from the concentrations required for the survival of your cells. Keeping your body healthy requires one continuous miracle of feedback loops.

Your emotions, both conscious and unconscious, help regulate the drives that keep your internal states intact and functional. All of our drives, instincts, and emotions are seamlessly woven into behaviors that help ensure that all of our internal systems are maintained. If you haven't eaten in two days, the sense of unease or anxiety that you feel, in addition to the discomfort emanating from your stomach, will motivate you to search for food. Your brain's primary task is to monitor and take care of your body, and it uses emotions to help it decide what to do next. There is no brain without a body—so the most important function of the brain is to maintain the body.

Emotions powerfully motivate our future and present behavior. For example, if we decide to stay in and study hard all night for an exam the next day, it may be more for the emotional state that we picture ourselves in years down the road, successful in our chosen field, than for the state we will be in after staying up all night. Delayed gratification is only physically delayed—you get to visualize, to imagine, albeit unconsciously, the emotional state that you think you will feel when you finally arrive at your goal. Imagining how you are going to feel when you pick up that diploma and show it to your parents allows you to project into the future, something that we humans are good at. (Maybe too good as too much attention is paid to the future and not enough to the present, not enough to the beautiful menagerie of birdsong around you.) Emotions help you decide what to do—your brain compares the imagined emotional state you will be in after flunking the exam versus getting an A and, hopefully, chooses the proper path. It is not as if you sat down and consciously appraised these two different imagined emotional states, gave them a numerical score, and chose the highest scorer—rather, your unconscious mind was influenced by the negative emotions generated by picturing failing the exam, and you then became consciously aware that something was amiss as you felt some anxiety and consciously interpreted that as the need to study. Perhaps you felt some guilt because you have so much work to do and you were out partying with friends; your unconscious evaluated the prospects of doing well on the exam, and the fear pathway was activated. By the time the fear reached your consciousness, you felt anxious, which then motivated you to buckle down and do some work.

To gain some perspective on emotions, it is helpful to trace them from less complex organisms. Studies on animals have revealed that there is no one emotion center in the brain; rather, each emotion has its own set of neuronal connections, which use some common pathways and some unique ones. Fear is one well-studied emotion that has been conserved across many species and whose pathway in the brain has been well worked out. Insights into fear can be gained by examining what happens with other species. For example, if you are a baby bird in a nest and see a large winged object flying overhead, you will respond with alarm and hide your head. Now this little chick has not been taught about eagles by its parents, nor has it ever seen one before, so its fear must derive from an innate program that has shown its usefulness over millennia. It's hard to be sure which, if any, mammals other than humans have consciousness, but most would agree that birds are not conscious of what they do. Therefore, the fear behavior exhibited by the chick is completely unconscious. Similarly, a laboratory rat will freeze immediately, as part of the fear response, if it sees a cat. Rats raised for research usually never see cats, so this is also an innate unconscious behavior. The similarities in the neuronal pathways of fear, from reptiles, birds, rats, and humans, have allowed researchers to carefully map out the pathways involved in our brains. We as humans are obviously different from other species, but many aspects, particularly the unconscious ones, are well conserved across species. One asks, if we do not invoke conscious feelings to understand emotions in animals, then why require them for all human emotions?

Darwin was one of the first to recognize the unconscious nature of many human emotional behaviors. He connected human emotional behavior to other species to show its evolutionary origins. Here is a beautiful example from Darwin's own life that he used to illustrate how involuntary, and outside of our conscious control, the fear reaction may be: "I put my face close to the thick glass-plate in front of a puff-ader in the Zoological Gardens with the firm determination of not starting back if the snake struck at me; but, as soon as the blow was struck, my resolution went for nothing, and I jumped a yard or two backwards with astonishing rapidity. My will and reason were powerless against the imagination of a danger which had never been experienced."

The important take-home message is that fear is part of an ancient emotional pathway whose job is to detect danger and produce a response that maximizes survival. Darwin jumped before he ever realized, consciously, why he moved. The emotional behavior of fear evolved long before conscious feelings evolved. Darwin's jump was part of that unconscious pathway. It is part of a highly orchestrated repertoire of defensive behaviors conserved across millions of years of evolutionary time.

What really happened when Darwin sat in front of that snake? As the snake moved to strike him, Darwin's eyes relayed the images of an object moving quickly toward his face to an old (by evolutionary time) area of the brain called the thalamus. The thalamus, in turn, quickly sent its signal to the amygdala, which has been called the hub of fear in the brain. The amygdala processed the rapid movement as dangerous and sent signals out to orchestrate the reflex of Darwin's jumping away from the snake. In addition, the amygdala sent signals to the hypothalamus, a deep part of our brains that connects to our heart, gut, blood vessels, sweat glands, and salivary glands. The system regulating internal body systems such as blood pressure, heart rate, breathing, sweating, and digestion is called the autonomic nervous system (ANS). These bodily functions are normally outside of conscious control but critical for life. Nerves reaching those different organs give rise to a racing heart, high blood pressure, sweaty palms, clammy hands and feet, a tight stomach, and a dry mouth.

The pathway from the thalamus to the amygdala has been called the "low road" by Joseph LeDoux and is considered a fast and dirty processing system. Dirty because this processing pathway doesn't always get it right: Darwin started to move away before he was sure what was attacking him. If the amygdala was wrong to worry because the glass was protecting Darwin, no harm done; but if the glass had not been there, it might have saved his life. Darwin's jump was an evolutionarily old reflexive response that occurred automatically, in spite of his resolve not to jump. Our first response to any potential threat involves the "low road." The "high road," which involves our cortex and conscious thoughts, gives us much more flexibility in our actions, and it cooperates with the "low road" to help humans reason and plan what to do next.

When we become consciously aware of our fear, we feel afraid or anxious. Although conscious fear or feelings are what many of us think of when we discuss fear, we don't need to have conscious feelings to have the emotion of fear generated within us. Our conscious awareness of our emotions is really the tip of the emotional iceberg. Darwin recognized that, and so did Freud.

Joseph LeDoux, a pioneer in research using animal models to elucidate the mechanisms of fear, writes, "And absence of awareness is the rule of mental life, rather than the exception, throughout the animal kingdom. If we do not need conscious feelings to explain what we would call emotional behavior in some animals, then we do not need them to explain the same behavior in humans. Emotional responses are, for the most part, generated unconsciously." It is worth repeating one line over again: "The absence of awareness is the rule of mental life."

The concept of the emotional unconscious is naturally quite counterintuitive. How could it be otherwise? Thus, it is not surprising that philosophers such as Descartes did not believe it exists. But just because your emotional unconscious is neither obvious nor widely appreciated does not mean it does not exist. If a moon of Jupiter passes behind Jupiter, you can no longer see it by telescope. At that moment your instrument of detection (the telescope and your visual pathway in the brain) is incapable of viewing a moon through the matter of Jupiter. How could your instruments of detection—your sight, smell, hearing, touch, and taste—visualize your emotional unconscious? They can't because they have not evolved for that function. Your senses have been adapted for learning about and assessing the outside world, not for telling you what is going on behind the scenes in the play we call your mind. If we limit ourselves to common sense and intuition, our interpretations of ourselves may be far off the mark. You can't "see" atoms with your unaided eyes, but there is no controversy now about whether they exist. We do not randomly leave the surface of earth in spite of our inability to comprehend, with our senses, what is behind that mysterious force called gravity.

By definition, you are only aware of your conscious emotions, and these have to be triggered by a pretty powerful unconscious emotion for you to become consciously aware. Most of the time your unconscious emotions guide your decision making in ways that remain hidden from view, so it is only on the basis of careful experimentation and clever reasoning that one can show unconscious emotions at work.

At their simplest, emotions represent preferences—one kind of movie gives you tender feelings and pulls you closer while another disgusts you, drives you away. To illustrate the emotional unconscious, it is helpful to review a few studies that show the mysterious ways that unconscious emotions influence the mind. Suppose you are riding up in the elevator with a new associate who is juggling papers, books, a computer, and coffee. You kindly offer to hold the cup of hot coffee for your new associate. Sometime later you are asked to judge how warm and friendly your new colleague is. (The new colleague was actually part of the experiment, but you were not aware of this.) It turns out that if you were holding hot coffee, you judged the elevator colleague to be warmer and friendlier than if you were holding cold coffee. Your brain sensed the warmth of the coffee and interwove that information with your conscious emotional evaluation of another human being. Your mind is literal in how it constructs evaluations.

The brain is fundamentally a sense-generating organ. It tries to pull together all the relevant data it receives from the outside world via hearing or sight or touch, or from the enormously complicated world hidden inside of you. Consider this—if you learn of your good score on an achievement test while sitting up straight, with good posture, you feel prouder of your accomplishment than if you were slumped over in your chair. (So mom and dad were right after all—it really does help to sit up straight!) Your brain received signals from your body that you were feeling healthy and strong because you had good posture—your mind took that assessment of your posture and conjoined it with your conscious feeling of pride, unbeknownst to your conscious you. Emotions and preferences are activated automatically all the time, and because they are unconscious, we are not aware of their influence on our thoughts and behavior. But your brain

knows that something is good or bad for you, making judgments, before it has identified what it is judging. Sounds absurd,
but there are good evolutionary reasons for it. Sometimes you
need to be fast to survive. It takes a lot of energy and time to
consciously weigh every decision—your unconscious emotions
provide a rapid first-response way of assessing the world.

Conscious fear, the feeling of fear that can be expressed ver-
bally to others, is actually the product of two neural systems.
The first is the unconscious fear behavior that helps us and the
rest of the animal kingdom escape danger, and the second is
the one that creates consciousness, the one that distinguishes us
from the frog that jumps into the pond when it sees us walking
by. Both neural systems are required for you to have the subjec-
tive experience of fear. The unconscious part of the system has
been around for many millions of years and has helped countless animals avoid being eaten. But by the time you "feel" afraid,
the unconscious fear system has been set in motion, and if it has
been caused by a snake, you have hopefully already jumped out
of the way. The unconscious system is faster and can remove you
from harm's way before you have any conscious idea of what you
are escaping from. The speed of the unconscious pathway is one
reason that it has been highly conserved across species. Those
fractions of a second can save your life, which is why the unconscious fear pathway is as strong in us as it is in a frog. The system
is separated anatomically from the neuronal pathway that allows
you to identify the nature of that projectile coming toward your
head. The pathway that allows you to recognize and categorize an object involves the cognitive, thinking, conscious part
of our brains, including the cortex. The conscious pathway has

longer physical connections within our brains; nerve pathways take fractions of a second to travel—they are not instantaneous, hence the slower reaction time to do something if you first have to think about it consciously. And in the heat of battle, your unconscious just might win the day.

Conscious emotional feelings arise in part from the signals that your amygdala sends to your cortex, allowing you to become consciously aware of your emotional unconscious. Antonio Damasio, the keen neurologic observer of how the mind works, describes feelings as a kind of sensor that detects when the world around you doesn't quite match what you expect. He emphatically states that "feelings, along with the emotions they come from, are not a luxury." He describes patients who, because of brain injuries, have lost their ability to have and feel emotions. Contrary to what most of us would assume, losing contact with your emotions is devastating. Patients can still perform well on an intelligence test—but they simply cannot manage in real life. When faced with the simplest of decisions, they become paralyzed with indecision. Everything we do, whether picking that box of cereal, deciding which movie to see, or choosing which career path to follow, requires emotional input. Feelings let us stay in touch with our bodies, with our selves. Damasio believes that feelings are not necessarily some elusive quality attached to an object; rather, they represent our brain's perception of what is going on inside our bodies. Your brain is continuously mapping and integrating information it receives from all the sensory receptors and nerves in the body. For example, if you are a diabetic and your blood sugar drops too low, you may feel nauseous, anxious, sweaty, and headachy. Sensors in your body will detect that not enough glucose is feeding your brain and other organs. You will feel unwell even though you may have no idea why. The unwell, anxious feeling is meant to protect you by motivating you to do something that makes you feel better, like eating.

In Damasio's model of emotion, feelings provide us with a window that opens directly onto a continually updated image of the state of the body. If a snake strikes at you, moments later you will "feel" scared, as you become aware of your body state— your trembling, your dry mouth, your pounding and racing heart, and your sweaty palms.

Emotions and the ANS are intricately intertwined. The ANS maintains the ideal internal body state and helps activate bodily systems to meet challenges and calm them down when action is no longer required. The body responds to emotional stress by activating a series of mechanisms known as the fight or flight response, which prepares us to either stand and fight or run from our attacker.

If your sailboat capsizes and the mast hits your shipmate in the head, your body needs to mount a coordinated response so you can save yourself and your friend. Your heart races, your muscles tense, and your blood pressure rises as you move blood away from areas like digestion to those areas that will help you right the sailboat. Your metabolism speeds up, your rate of breathing increases, the pupils of your eyes dilate, and the arteries in your arms and legs constrict so that less blood will be lost if you are injured. You feel the urge to urinate and move the bowels, and you begin to sweat. If the emergency is real, then this coordinated response is good. But if the emergency has long passed or never was, and you still have some of the same symptoms, then this is an unhealthy reaction to chronic stress.

LET US RETURN to our experiments on facial expression and emotion. We have seen earlier in this chapter how changes in facial expression can alter conscious emotions. But we have also just learned how crucial and influential our unconscious emotions are for our well-being and for decision making. Can you show that altering a facial expression alters unconscious emotions, including your ANS?

Researchers decided to ask whether altered facial expressions could affect parts of the body that are normally completely involuntary and out of conscious control, such as heart rate. They asked their experimental subjects to contract precise sets of facial muscles to create expressions of surprise, fear, disgust, anger, happiness, and sadness. In order not to bias the experiment through the power of suggestion, they were clever in the way they instructed their subjects. Instead of asking the volunteers participating in the experiment to look fearful, for example, they asked them to "raise your brows and pull them together, raise your upper eyelids" and "now stretch your lips horizontally, back toward your ears." In a separate session after a break, they asked the same volunteers to recall an experience that frightened them. By measuring involuntary changes in the ANS—heart rate, blood pressure, sweating—during the two parts of the experiment, they found that moving facial muscles produced more involuntary fearful reactions than attempts by subjects to relive a past frightening experience. They found the same remarkable difference for the other fundamental emotions:

happiness, anger, sadness, disgust, and surprise. Their results showed that simply moving our faces can have more powerful direct effects on our hearts and vascular systems than trying to relive emotional events in our minds.

How does movement of the face actually cause emotion to be felt? Some theorize that the brain recognizes the pattern of activity in the facial muscles or the movement of the overlying skin. We know that every muscle can send signals to the brain via the peripheral nerves. The brain would be continuously aware of which muscles of facial expression were active at any given time. Recent studies have shown that imitating angry facial expressions is associated with neural activation in regions such as the amygdala. As we have seen, the amygdala is a key player for our emotional brain as it evaluates emotionally salient information that it receives from a variety of sources. This region is also activated when we look at a fearful or sad face. The amygdala in turn has strong reciprocal connections to the hypothalamus and brain stem regions, which are involved in control of autonomic functions such as heart rate, blood pressure, and sweating. Thus, a pathway has been found to help explain how facial expressions could alter autonomic functions. Others propose that the motor cortex (the part of the brain that signals the muscles to contract) connects directly to the emotion-generating center of the brain.

Another theory suggests that facial muscles control the flow of venous (cooler) blood to the brain, indirectly affecting brain blood temperature, which controls the release and synthesis of neurotransmitters. Higher brain temperature has been associated with more negative feelings. Perhaps the metaphors "boiling mad," "hotheaded," and "cool as a cucumber" are not metaphors at all.

What we do know is that while facial expressions are not necessary to create emotions, they are sufficient to generate emotional feelings. Indeed, it has been observed that voluntary true smiles, smiles that include the eyes, correspond with increases in left prefrontal cortex activity. Similarly, researchers have found that voluntary expressions of sadness and fear result in decreases in left prefrontal cortex activity and increases in right prefrontal cortex activity, a pattern associated with anxiety and depression.

Researchers asked whether they could see a difference in fMRI-visualized activation of the amygdala by treating normal subjects with Botox injected into their frown muscle. Those subjects who received Botox injected into their frown muscles were then asked to try and make an angry face. They found that Botox inhibited the subjects' ability to activate the amygdala by making an angry face. This was the first direct demonstration of facial muscle feedback affecting the activation of a part of the brain that is crucial for emotion.

CHAPTER 8

EMBODIED EMOTION

"I had the blues so bad it put my face in a permanent frown, but
I'm feeling so much better I can cakewalk into town."

—Taj Mahal

WHEN I FIRST heard Taj Mahal's song, it stopped me dead
in my tracks. Here this great musician was describing
how he felt so despondent that it gave him a frown on his face
that never went away. But I beg to differ with his explanation
of the sequence of events; I suggest that the permanent frown
helped give him the blues, not the reverse.

We know there are specific facial expressions for many emotions. But is there a face to match a depressed internal state? Do
you need to look depressed in some way, shape, or form to feel
depressed? Does depression only exist in your head, or does it
require some physical expression in your body and face? Can you
laugh and smile with abandon, be the life of the party, and still
suffer terribly inside? Perhaps, but I suspect that it is more than
likely that when you are acting the part of the life of the party,

you are not depressed at that moment—even if you feel sullen and sad later on that evening. Although some of us may show a poker face while suffering deeply inside, many who are severely depressed display a face that is characteristic of depression.

Here is Darwin's description of people suffering from excessive grief:

> The eyebrows not rarely are rendered oblique, which is due to the inner ends being raised. This produces peculiarly-formed wrinkles on the forehead, which are very different from those of a simple frown; though in some cases a frown alone may be present. The corners of the mouth are drawn downwards, which is so universally recognized as a sign of being out of spirits, that it is almost proverbial.

Now grief is not depression—it is a normal reaction to a loss. But persistent grief often evolves into depression. It usually helps to study the extremes of anything you wish to understand—it is easier to detect the salient and crucial features of any phenomenon because all the random variations in nature are less distracting when you see large differences. Darwin recognized this, so to further understand this facial expression, he sought descriptions of patients who had become so depressed, so melancholic that they were confined to asylums for the insane. It is important to remember that during Darwin's time, no viable therapy for depression existed. There were no drugs and no talking therapy to stop one from descending into a state of complete hopelessness. One was powerless to do anything but observe the entire natural history of depression. Here Darwin describes one severe depressive: "a widow, aged 51, fancied that she had lost all her viscera, and that her whole body was empty. She wore an expression of great distress.... The grief muscles were permanently contracted, and the upper eyelids arched. This condition lasted for months; she then recovered, and her countenance resumed its natural expression."

So distinctive was this special facial expression seen in depression in the 1800s that doctors began calling it "omega melancholium," defined in a psychiatric dictionary as "a wrinkle (between the eyebrows) in the shape of the last letter of the Greek alphabet, the omega ['Ω], assumed to indicate a state of melancholy." Physicians' awareness of this facial expression may have diminished over the past 150 years, but the expression remains a powerful indicator of suffering to this day. The face and its expressions, however, are not part of our current

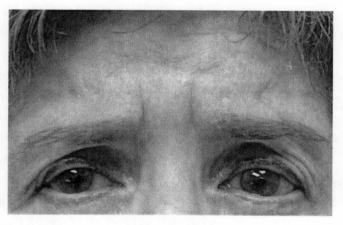

Figure 8.1   The expression of Omega Melancholium

diagnostic criteria for depression. Facial expressions have sort of disappeared from current teachings about mental illness. Physicians of yesteryear paid much more attention to the face when they had fewer treatments and fewer pressures along with more time to observe the natural history of disease.

Darwin makes the distinction between the persistent action of the grief muscles in the insanely depressed (what we now call major depression with psychotic features) and the momentary contraction of these same muscles as an expression of displeasure or frustration.

"I once watched a young woman and a youth, both in the highest spirits, eagerly talking with extraordinary rapidity, and I noticed that, as often as the young lady could not get her words out fast enough, and was cut off by the youth, her eyebrows moved obliquely upwards, and rectangular furrows formed on her forehead. She thus hoisted this flag of distress half-a-dozen times in the course of a few minutes."

We have seen how the facial muscles are intimately involved in the generation of feelings. And we have seen how some individuals can look depressed. But there is a long road to travel from looking and feeling angry or sad today and becoming depressed tomorrow. Just because your facial expressions are involved with the creation of feelings doesn't prove that the facial muscles are involved with long-term changes of mood such as depression. What then is the experimental evidence that your face can actually play a role in depression?

Researchers asked a simple question: If you think a sad thought, does that lead to changes in facial muscle activity?

To answer this question, they attached electrodes to the surface of the skin to measure underlying muscle activity, a process called electromyography (EMG). They asked their subjects to think about something that made them sad while they continuously monitored the muscles that govern frowns and smiles. The researchers found increases in frown activity when subjects thought sad thoughts. If their subjects tried to re-experience sad feelings along with sad thoughts, frown activity increased even more. Conversely, if subjects tried thinking about something that made them feel happy and tried to re-experience the feeling, they frowned less while smiling more. Interestingly, none of the changes in muscle activity was visible to the naked eye; there was no frown or smile to be seen when subjects thought sad or happy thoughts. So the emotional valence, the positivity or negativity of your thinking, can be expressed by your facial muscles without your or others' even being aware of it.

It may be that what you can discern from looking at someone's face is really just a small part of what is actually happening to the facial muscles; there are changes in facial muscle activity occurring all the time, but only the largest changes can be easily seen without special tools.

In another study, subjects were asked to read a series of statements that were designed to change their mood. For example, to feel happier, they would repeat to themselves, "I feel so vivacious and efficient today—sitting on top of the world." Or, to create depressive feelings, they would say, "At times I've been so tired and discouraged that I went to sleep rather than face important problems." A large body of literature has demonstrated that the simple act of repetitively reading such statements temporarily leads to genuine changes in mood. How could that work?

Recent studies have shown that comprehending a sentence calls on the same neuronal systems that you normally use to perceive, perform, or feel the action you have just read about. So reading a happy story actually causes you to activate some of the same parts of the brain that would be activated if you were in the story.

Even reading a single word can change your facial expression. In one study, subjects were asked to decide, yes or no, whether a word was associated with an emotion. They tested the premise of the experiment by trying different kinds of words like "water" or "wood," which are neutral, versus more emotional words like "slime" or "stench." If subjects only had to tell whether a word was capitalized, no facial muscles were activated, even if the word was an emotionally laden one, like "death." But if they were asked whether "slug" was related to an emotion, the facial muscles used in disgust were activated (most people apparently find slugs disgusting). Only if they had to decode the meaning of the word did the facial muscles become active. By contrast, your brain could decide whether a word was capitalized without any reference to your face. Your brain wants to involve your face to help it understand what emotional words really mean. During the time it took (less than three seconds) for participants to decide whether the word "slug" was related to an emotion, the facial muscles normally used when we act disgusted were activated.

We have seen that researchers have shown that the simple act of repetitively reading a statement such as "I am sitting on top of the world" actually makes you feel better. The finding that making self-referential statements can actually change feelings is consistent with the theory of cognitive therapy for depression. The essence of cognitive behavioral therapy for depression is the concept that irrational thoughts and beliefs, a pessimistic outlook on life, a tendency to focus on negative events, and a negative self-assessment promote psychological ill health. Cognitive therapy helps the depressed patient change the pessimistic ideas, negative expectations, and overly critical self- evaluations that help create and sustain depression. Depressives think awful things about themselves and their future. Psychologists use cognitive therapy as a way of helping them understand and alter the distortions in thinking that are contributing to depression. And suppose that things are objectively terrible—then a little self-deception might help.

Let us see how the experiment involved the facial muscles. Subjects read sad and negative statements while the scientists recorded their facial muscle activity. The correlation was strong: Reading more depressive statements led to greater increases in frown muscle activity. And people retained the expressions for some time after the experiment ended. By contrast, happy statements led to rapid increases in smile muscle activity, which promptly returned to baseline during rest periods. The experiment suggests that in order to help our minds understand what we are reading, our brains re-create at least part of the emotion, in this case the facial muscle component, to embody the statement read. This concept of embodied emotion has been confirmed by many psychologists. Our minds can't really understand what is happening around us without activating some of the same neurons that would perform the action in real life.

Antonio Damasio, the theorist of how the mind works, states, "It is not only the separation between brain and mind that is mythical: the separation between mind and body is probably just as fictional. The mind is embodied, in the full sense of the term, not just embrained."

The experiments also suggest that we may have more difficulty in dismissing negative than neutral or positive thoughts. A negative thought stays around in our minds longer, at least as represented by the muscles involved, than does a positive thought. In practical terms, you may have to smile and laugh for some time to reverse a negative thought. These experiments suggest that the changes in facial muscle activity observed could contribute to depression by feeding back to the brain.

The Botox Test

William S. was a young man who came to my office to have a mole removed by one of my partners. Then he told me the poignant story of his struggle with depression. He recounted,

> For the past 13 years I have suffered from severe clinical depression, obsessive compulsive disorder, panic attacks, as well as bouts of severe anxiety. At the age of 14, I was diagnosed with clinical depression that had rendered me very suicidal (to the point where I would break down and cry if I saw

a knife or a pair of scissors, in fear that I might use them to end my life).

By the time I was 20, I was in the process of changing psychiatrists because my depression was worsening, and my psychiatrist could no longer help me the way I needed to be helped. During the transition from one psychiatrist to another, I experienced a severe panic attack (it felt like I was having a heart attack and also felt like I was experiencing something trying to rip out of my chest). My panic attack lasted two weeks. When I finally got to see the new psychiatrist, she instructed me to admit myself into the hospital, and she also gave me some medications to alleviate the anxiety, the panic attacks, and the depression. For the next month, I was getting loaded up on and maxed out on 20 or more antidepressants, an antipsychotic, and a Valium a day because I had hit rock bottom. For six months I stayed that way, still going to therapy once, sometimes twice a week. During those six months I was so sedated, my parents had to shake me hard to get me to wake up.

By 2003, I had hit rock bottom again, I even said out loud that if someone didn't do something, I would overdose on my medications. I was sent into the hospital for four or five days. Literally one day after my release, I was having panic attacks and severe depression again.

Within months following my third hospitalization (I was so stressed out, anxious, depressed), I was declared "Disabled" by the state. For almost two years now, I have been on disability, and I work very few hours a month because of my anxiety level and the depression. Within the past eight months, I had another hospitalization (number four), and it got so bad for me that the doctor directed me to get ECT (electroconvulsive therapy). Over the past summer, I had 16 ECT procedures, which rendered me basically useless. They caused fatigue, headaches, memory loss, etc. The two weeks following my last treatment I was praying I wouldn't wake up because I was so bad off. My psychiatrist said that I was running out of options because I'd done most of the SSRI medications, I'd had an unsuccessful ECT experience, and I was still floundering. She sent me home with a new prescription (Prozac).

I was in Dr. Finzi's dermatology office for a mole removal procedure, and I was watching a video playing on the television in the waiting room about "Botox and Depression." There were several news reports, a client's testimony about the positive effects of the Botox treatment, and even Dr. Finzi explaining his theory. Based on my knowledge of psychology, I thought this was the doctor's scam to make a few extra bucks at the expense of ill people like myself. After my doctor had removed my mole, I asked him about Dr. Finzi's "Botox-Depression Theory," and two minutes later I was talking to Dr. Finzi. He explained the procedure and the physiology behind his theory. Still skeptical about the procedure, I went home to think about what I wanted to do.

"On a scale of one to ten, ten being the best and one being the worst, I was a one. It was either put Dr. Finzi's Botox test to the test or die. The next day, I made an emergency visit to Dr. Finzi to receive his Botox injections.

It has been a little over a month since my Botox injections. Several people have noticed a very big change in me. I am more energized, and I am smiling. I hold myself (my posture) more confidently, I was told.

What is more amazing is how I'm feeling. I am happier than I have been in a long time. But I wanted to make sure the "Botox test" was actually working. It just so happened that I didn't fill my prescription for Prozac until after I had the Botox injections.

Three days after my Botox injection (still on the same medications I was on when I was at my last "rock bottom"), I was
supposed to start taking Prozac. By the third day I was feeling
fine. I decided to hold off on the Prozac. Days became weeks,
and now, over a month later, I don't feel the need to take Prozac.
Although I am not cured of my depression, I think the Botox
test has worked; I don't wish every day that I would never wake
up. I smile more often, I have more energy, I don't cry as much
as I used to. On a scale of one to ten, I would have to say I am
now a five or six.

Now I certainly don't advise anyone to ignore the instructions
of their treating physicians, as this young man did. But I have
not paraphrased his words because editing can change meaning,
and there is nothing more direct than the patient's own words.
William's story suggests to me that botulinum toxin treatment
of the frown should also be tried on those who are profoundly
depressed and incapacitated by their disease, not just those who
don't feel well but manage to get by. We are only at the beginning of research in this area; we do not know who will respond
and who will not.

MORE THAN 30 years ago, before the selective serotonin re-uptake
inhibitors (SSRIs) were in use, a few researchers began work to
try and understand the relationship between depression and
the muscles of facial expression. They posed the question: Do
depressed individuals have facial muscle activity that differs from
that of normal subjects? To help answer this question, scientists
asked depressed and normal subjects to simply think about what

they do in a typical day. At the same time, they recorded facial muscle activity by a procedure called electromyography (EMG). Depressed subjects were found to activate the frown muscles while normal subjects activated the smile muscles. The differences in facial muscle activity were not visible to the naked eye. They also found that depressed subjects had an abnormal facial muscle response to happy thoughts. Unlike their normal counterparts, depressed subjects had little increase in smile muscle activity with happy thoughts and feelings. What would normally trigger smile muscle activation in most of us did not do so in people who were depressed. I use the term "smile muscle activation" rather than "smiles" because I stress again that nothing these researchers observed would have been visible to you or me by just looking at the study subject. All the activity was happening out of view. Some of their depressed patients even had abnormal increases in frown muscle activity in response to happy thoughts. These studies were important in showing that frown and smile muscles do not act normally when one is depressed.

We have seen much evidence to suggest the role our facial muscles play in the generation of our emotions, moods, and feelings. We know from cognitive psychology that prolonged sad thinking may precipitate depression. Research has shown that sad thoughts increase frown activity and, conversely, increased frown activity increases sad thoughts. Depressed individuals have abnormal facial muscle activity. The question to be answered is how much of a role facial muscles play in the generation and maintenance of depression.

To help answer this question, it would be useful if we could physically prevent a patient from frowning. We would want to design a drug that is safe, specific, easy to use, and highly effective at preventing frown muscle activity. When this idea came to me some time ago, I realized that such a drug was already widely available and I had been giving it to patients for years.

I have treated depressed patients who showed no salient visible frown, but who, subsequent to receiving Botox, felt a marked improvement in their emotional state. The frown muscles don't have to be visibly contracting. Your muscle tone might be so strong that your face bounces back into a smile right away. You might be frowning, but there might be enough time between the contractions that a permanent frown doesn't form. The contractions of those frown muscles, though far apart, are still sending negative emotional signals back to the brain. I believe that the brain is measuring the strength of the frown muscle contraction, weighing it against the strength of the smile, which can be seen as the pulse of the positive feelings of happiness—and then producing an emotion. I call this *emotional proprioception*—just as your mind tracks the smallest movements of your hands or feet, it is tracking those little muscles that control your face. Then we have the tricky thing about perception. It may sound too obvious to say, but in our everyday interactions, we don't see what is going on in someone else's brain. We don't see how the brain decides what emotion to make us feel. We do see each other's faces all the time, so we assume emotions are interwoven with our facial muscles. What we don't see is the messages going up to the brain, which assesses them and then passes down emotional signals. The brain can't have feelings in some ether—the feelings need some embodiment, and the face plays an important role.

I suggest that every time you frown, you are sending an impulse back to your brain: "This is unpleasant." "Get me out of here." I'm not happy." If the noise is horrible and the smell is foul, you're going to start frowning. And your mind will be told that it needs to move away. In people suffering from depression, though, it is not so easy to just move away, to jump out of the skin. Human mental health is influenced by the agility of your facial muscles.

One way to visualize it is to think of a scale where you are balancing frown muscle tension against smile muscle tension. You can feel better by applying more weight to the smile side or less weight to the frown side.

The brain measures the tempo. Vivace, allegro, lentissimo, larghissimo. The brain is continually, unconsciously measuring the tempo of the face of either the positive side (your smile) or the negative side (your frown muscles). It's as if you are being constantly surveyed, only it is your brain watching the physical you. Our brain uses our body—in this case, our facial muscles—as a yardstick, a reference, for our emotional states. The brain's emotional thermometer measures the activity of our facial muscles and any deviation from their most recent activity. Our cognitive unconscious is always busy—but we only become aware when something important bubbles up to the surface, into our consciousness.

When there is no tension in the frown muscles, when those muscles have been temporarily frozen with Botox, there is no negative feedback to report back to the brain. The lack of this negativity then creates a tremendously significant positive effect on our brain's assessment of our mental state. Botox prevents the frown muscle from contracting, as if there were no nerve signals to it. If the motor nerve in a muscle in your arm suddenly gets killed, your arm will atrophy. When the body doesn't register muscle tension in the frown, positive progression takes place in the mind.

In trying to answer the chicken or the egg question, which came first, the facial expression or the feedback to the brain, we must realize it is a loop and perhaps they simply developed together.

Botox Overcomes a Depression

Simone was a volunteer subject in my study. While she did not exhibit any pronounced frown lines before I gave her the Botox injections, she did say that she had "suffered from depression for a long time." At times in the past, she had been in therapy with a psychologist and had taken Prozac, Wellbutrin, and Effexor. Simone claimed that she never felt any relief from the pharmaceuticals. When she took my study's initial diagnostic exam, Simone was surprised by how high her score was. A high score on the Beck Depression Inventory (BDI) test means you are feeling quite depressed. This test helps physicians assess how depressed someone is.

"It showed even more significant depression than I thought I had," she told me. "For me I guess depression had been a chronic condition, and, as with other chronic conditions, it waxes and wanes. And so there would be times when it was very clear that I was very depressed. There were other times, just like anything, I kind of grow accustomed to living with it. And so it really took me filling out this diagnostic and saying wow, you know, my symptoms are pretty significant."

After I gave her the Botox in her grief muscle, she said,

> My reaction was not dramatic. And it was not overnight. It wasn't like I went to bed feeling miserable one day and I woke up the next day and I was like, oh, I feel great. I went and did the follow-up. I took the same diagnostic that I had taken at the outset of the study and I was amazed at the difference in my scores. It was a dramatic improvement. The reality is that I was feeling lighter. It's almost like when you carry around a weight for a long time, you don't consciously realize you're carrying a weight until you set it down and you feel lighter. My feeling is that when people are suffering over a long period of time, they have to adapt—it's like people who deal with chronic physical pain. If they didn't find a way to cope with that, they couldn't survive. So they survive with this physical pain, and they somehow become acclimated to it. It doesn't mean that it's not there. It just means that it's not a part of their conscious experience. I think I had just kind of grown acclimated to carrying that weight around....After the Botox, I started doing things that were important to me, reconnecting with friends, becoming more social, becoming more spiritual again.

Simone had struggled with alcohol and drugs in the past. She had started seeing a therapist in high school and then stopped until college. "And then I went on a wild, I guess I would term it self-medicating, episode." It was the early 1980s, and she was living in New York's Greenwich Village. She eventually went to Alcoholics Anonymous for her excessive drinking, and though she has remained sober now for 21 years, she stopped going to meetings. A year before she entered the study, she had relapsed on abusing pain medication, mainly Percodan. Her nine-year-old son used to say Mommy would sleep all the time. "But after getting my Botox treatment, I recommitted to going to a lot more [Alcoholic Anonymous] meetings. You know, making sure that I was really taking care of that aspect of my life. I stopped abusing pain killers. I got a great new job.

"The only thing that changed is that I had Botox, and therefore I must attribute feeling better to Botox. However, what I can say is that to me it's highly plausible that it was an impact and that over time as I continued to get it, I haven't slipped into any episodes of depression."

Simone showed no visible frown lines at rest before I gave her the injections, proving again that the psychological effect is not due to improved appearance. We have found that you don't need to have a visible frown to get improvement in mood after Botox injections. (As we saw earlier, some people can have quite a bit of frown muscle activity—yet not show a permanent frown that is visible. I believe that it is a bit like blood pressure—it is hard to tell from the outside what is going on inside of us.)

ONE OF MY patients, Stacey, provides a perfect case history to help support the principle that looking better after the frown lines are removed is not the reason for the relief in mental depression that follows. She is a 52-year-old office manager at a design firm in Maryland. Stacey had initially come to my office for the treatment of skin cancer. I immediately noticed the deep lines between her eyebrows.

She relates that I told her, "You have a pretty bad frown." She says, "I was just in tears, I felt so bad. I always felt bad.... I wasn't happy in general no matter what I did. I have a nice life. I have a great husband. I have great kids. But I would always tend to look at the sad side—I would never be glad about anything."

Stacey had been on several medications, including Paxil and Wellbutrin, which, she says, might have worked to make her non-suicidal or non-depressed. "But I wasn't cheerful or happy or positive.... I think I've tried every kind of antidepressant, and nothing worked. They just didn't agree with me. They made me feel very stoic. I didn't care. I just didn't care about anything. I was never very happy. Even with antidepressants. Maybe I wasn't depressed but I wasn't happy. I was more of a pessimist than an optimist, you know what I mean?"

I told her about my work on treating depression with Botox injections into the frown muscles. So we decided to go ahead with a Botox injection into her corrugator muscle.

"I never thought in a million years that I would be getting Botox, never! I've never believed in any of that stuff. I'm not one to do plastic surgery, and I thought people who did that were vain."

A little over a week after she had the Botox, Stacey progressively felt more positive. She was happier—she was simply cheerful. She no longer felt as if she were always in the gutter, no longer sad and overwhelmed, depressed about life in general, as she subtly had been for many years. In a follow-up interview, I told her, "I can see you're smiling, laughing."

She replied, "Everybody says that. There's gotta be a connection.... I just feel so much more in control of my life somehow.

I don't know. I know I'm doing a good job. I got a nice raise. I got a nice bonus."

Like many of my patients, after a period of time as the Botox wore off, Stacey started to feel her mental strength weaken, even though her frown lines had not yet returned to her face. "I feel it's wearing off inside," she said. "I'm starting to get a little bit like I used to be and it's scaring me.... I'm slipping back. I'm starting to cry. It's there all the time. I'm really tired when I get home from work. I get depressed. And it's not as much as I used to be. Believe me I wasn't a believer in any of this stuff."

So I gave Stacey another Botox treatment on her frown muscles, and she returned to her solid self again after a week.

HERE ARE THE reflections on Botox of Eva Ritvo, MD, the vice chairman of psychiatry at the University of Miami:

My interest in Botox has been building for some time, but it was sparked higher by an experience I had recently after trying my own Botox injection. Not long after I had it, I went to see the new film about the late, great Michael Jackson, *This Is It*. Now, I grew up on the same street as the Jackson family; I saw some of the early parts of Michael's story play out. So this movie affected me deeply. At the end, I wanted to cry at the tragedy of this brilliantly gifted man's life ending so early. But I couldn't. For some reason, the paralysis of the muscles in my glabellar area resulting from the injections of botulinum toxin A rendered me totally unable to cry. Curious. But even more surprisingly, when I couldn't cry, I quickly stopped feeling sad. I left the movie with my girlfriend, who was feeling very down, and I felt so odd that I couldn't find those emotions. I was ready to go on to the next activity. Sadness was nowhere to be found. It was as if the emotion came up, couldn't be expressed, and so went away. Very curious indeed. Over the next weeks, I had many sad moments and again was unable to cry. The emotions lingered a bit but felt "unreal" and disconnected. These odd moments made me wonder about a few things. First, had other women (or men) experienced what I had experienced? Second, could Botox be an adjunctive treatment for depression?

Depression is a notoriously fickle state of mind. One can be depressed for months on end, and then, as mysteriously as it entered one's life, it may depart as one regains normal desire, ability, and mood. Since Botox wears off after several months, one might expect that some patients would find themselves falling back under the spell of depression as the frown muscle activity reemerges. This is precisely what I have seen in a number of patients, with stories similar to those of Stacey and Simone. Repeat treatment of the frown muscles with botulinum toxin then tips the scale back in the happier direction.

SOME OF US are surprised that muscle tension in the face can profoundly impact psychological health. But there is ample evidence found in a widely used technique—yoga. We know, for example, that the brain monitors our breathing. If it finds that the muscles are contracting too rapidly, it will tell them to slow down. Conversely, if you run up the stairs, you will breathe faster to compensate for all the oxygen your muscles are using for your climb. A yogi reverses this sequence by training his body to slow down his breathing to harmonize his body and mind.

Lamaze breathing for childbirth is another example of focusing on breathing to help soothe the mind during a time of intense pain and stress.

If one area of the body is important to our physical and psychological health, then one might expect other cultures to place emphasis on that area. That is precisely what we see in Eastern cultures. Hindis and Buddhists believe that the "third eye" lies in a spot between the eyebrows. To them, the area between the eyebrows is a powerful spiritual, psycho-energetic center. It is called the "third eye" for it is the window, the portal, through which a student receives—sees—his guru's telepathic communication. The area is believed to contain a pathway to the mind, to the spirit, to one's complete psychic being. Yogis strive to open this area up internally. Is it just a coincidence that this is where we inject Botox to help alleviate depression?

What is remarkable is that the inhibition of the frown muscles and stimulation of smiling and laughter are precisely what is taught in some yoga classes. These are the words of one yoga instructor:

"Inhale: and raise your eyebrows as much as you can.

Exhale: and draw them together in a deep frown.

Repeat a few more times, pushing the eyebrows higher and lower each time.

Inhale: close your eyes and place the fingertips of both hands on the center of your forehead.

Exhale: stroke the fingers out to the edges of the temples, wiping away any last tension.

Repeat a few more times and then feel the muscles of your forehead relaxing and spreading out.

Now smile and take the corners of your mouth as wide as you can: imagine or say out loud the letter sound 'eeeee.'

Then purse your lips and imagine, or say out loud, the sound 'oouu' as in 'you.'

Repeat a few more times, stretching and squeezing the muscles more each time.

Then relax, and if you haven't burst out laughing, feel how much more relaxed, plump, and well-nourished the muscles of the face feel. Notice how much of the tension in the face and jaw has melted away. If you have been laughing, then enjoy the rejuvenating effect that has had on you too!"

SCIENTIFIC ADVANCES LIVE or die by data from independent experiments replicating the initial findings. Since our initial study was published, there have been several reported that firmly support it.

Researchers compared the mood of patients attending a cosmetic surgery clinic before and after they received either Botox or fillers to enhance their looks. The group that received Botox had a happier mood relative to the controls who received other cosmetic procedures.

Another group of researchers asked what effect Botox had on self-esteem and quality of life in normal individuals. In their double-blind, randomized, placebo-controlled trial with 100 participants, Botox recipients had statistically significant improvements in both self-esteem and quality of life measures.

The previous two studies showed that Botox seemed to lift the mood of normal individuals. But what about patients who are depressed?

The gold standard in clinical medicine is the randomized, double-blind, placebo-controlled clinical trial. Axel Wollmer is a psychiatrist who holds the distinction of being the first to publish a clinical trial of Botox as a treatment for depression that meets the gold standard. Enlisting a team of researchers in both Switzerland and Germany, Wollmer and his associate Tillman Kruger randomly assigned depressed patients to receive either Botox or a placebo injection into their frown muscles. They recruited people who had, for the most part, failed standard treatments for their depression. They then monitored their patients over a 16-week period to assess how their depressive symptoms were affected by the injections.

Compared to the placebo, the Botox-injected group had a highly statistically significant improvement in depressive symptoms that was seen throughout the course of the study. Six weeks after treatment with Botox, patients experienced a 47 percent reduction in scores that qualified them as depressed, compared with a 9 percent reduction for those who received the placebo. More than half of Botox patients responded, compared with only 13 percent of placebo patients. These numbers are remarkable. At every time point, the Botox patients felt better than the placebo group. With every psychiatric test of depression, the Botox patients improved. They were also able to show that treatment response did not depend on patients' thinking that they looked better. In fact, one of their patients who went into remission actually disliked the change in her facial appearance.

There are at least two other ongoing clinical trials. Jason Reichenberg and Michelle Magid are a husband and wife team, dermatologist and psychiatrist, based in Austin, Texas. They are conducting a double-blind, placebo-controlled crossover study of Botox for depression. After my initial study was published, Reichenberg showed the work to his wife. Their enthusiasm for a new idea led to the hard work to secure funding for a trial. Hopefully this open-minded couple will be publishing their results around the time that this book comes out. I am also finishing up a collaborative trial with Norman Rosenthal that we hope to present shortly.

WE HAVE SPECULATED on the mechanism by which Botox may help depression. Is there any recent research that gives more insight?

First, what happens in the brain when we are depressed, and what happens after our depression goes into remission from taking a standard SSRI?

Researchers asked whether effective antidepressant treatment influenced the activation of the amygdala in response to seeing a fearful facial expression. They found a highly significant correlation between those patients who experienced a remission of their depression after treatment with paroxetine, an SSRI, and those who had a reduction in amygdala activation after seeing a fearful face. Only those patients who were no longer depressed, and not the group of patients who took the paroxetine but were still depressed, showed the association. Those patients whose depression did not improve after paroxetine treatment had no change in their fear pathway. Their amygdalas were still just as reactive to fearful faces. The fear hub, the amygdala, definitely seems implicated in part of the depression pathway.

Does Botox have any involvement in this pathway?

A separate group of researchers asked whether they could see a difference in fMRI visualized activation of the amygdala by treating non-depressed subjects with Botox injected into their frown muscle. Those subjects who received Botox into their frown muscles were then asked to try and make an angry face. They found that Botox inhibited the subjects' ability to activate the amygdala by making an angry face. This was the first direct demonstration that Botox treatment of the frown muscle could affect the activation of a part of the brain, the amygdala, whose activity has been implicated in depression.

It will be exciting to examine brain activity in those depressed patients who go into remission after Botox treatment. Researchers hope that this will give us more insight into the mechanism by which Botox helps depression.

CHAPTER 9

LAUGHTER

"Laughter is the sun that drives winter from the human face."
—Victor Hugo

ONE MORNING MY daughter and I had to rush to catch the morning school bus. My daughter's mouth was really hurting from the previous day's orthodontic trauma. The wires pulling her teeth together had just been tightened, and her gums had swollen to almost cover the metal. Every breakfast morsel evoked a fleeting but pronounced eyebrow frown, as her mouth rebelled against eating. Her school bus was arriving in just five minutes. The pressure of having to eat too quickly made her frown even more. As we dashed out the door on this cold, damp February day, her forehead provided ongoing commentary about this thoroughly unpleasant situation.

We drove to the bottom of the hill and parked, and as we waited in the car, we both spied a middle-aged man with a large floppy potbelly tiptoe gingerly in his bare feet toward the object of his desire—a dew-soaked newspaper. He wore only large yellow underwear. I turned to my daughter, whose face beamed with an enormous smile that quickly turned into laughter. The incongruity of the situation combined with the release of tension from her pain and the rush to catch the bus provided the perfect setting for a display of happy emotions, smiling, and laughter.

Laughter looks so natural, so simple, that we usually take it for granted. But even more than smiling, laughter is a human behavior that has only recently opened itself up to scientific scrutiny. As always, if you want a good description of a scientific phenomenon, turn to Charles Darwin.

> Joy, when intense, leads to various purposeless movements—to dancing about, clapping the hands, stamping, &c., and to loud laughter. Laughter seems primarily to be the expression of mere joy or happiness. We clearly see this in children at play, who are almost incessantly laughing. With young persons past childhood, when they are in high spirits, there is always much meaningless laughter. The laughter of the gods is described by Homer as "the exuberance of their celestial joy after their daily banquet." A man smiles—and smiling, as we shall see, graduates into laughter—at meeting an old friend in the street, as he does at any trifling pleasure, such as smelling a sweet perfume.

I am not sure exactly what Darwin meant by "meaningless laughter." Perhaps he was making the distinction between the specific content of words versus the generic quality of laughter. But, hopefully, by the end of this chapter, you will respectfully disagree with Darwin and find laughter to be a meaningful activity. Human behavior may be cryptic, but it "means" something. There must be strong evolutionary reasons that all known societies of humans laugh.

THE STUDY OF laughter presents some of the same difficulties as the study of bird flight indoors. Once you capture a bird and house it in a small cage, you are not going to observe much flying. You might even come to the erroneous conclusion that birds don't fly much, the same way we think that some animals are stupid when they do repetitive behaviors at the zoo. (But if you locked me in a concrete cage, without distractions, I might bang my head against that same wall.)

One fundamental theme of laughter, which is sometimes lost in all the complexity that laughter can engender, is its positive role for our health and happiness. Laughter is a unique combination of a facial expression with a distinct vocalization. The real benefits of laughter usually get dismissed because we instinctively do not take laughter seriously. In addition, because laughter can be seen in a negative context, we forget what an overwhelmingly positive emotion it can, and should, be. I shall review some of its main features, including those negative roles that have skewed some views of laughter, before we return to its important role for our well-being.

Anyone who has children knows that laughter starts early in life—it is one of the first vocalizations that infants make—between two and six months of age. To hear your baby laugh, that magic of a chuckling infant, well, sometimes I think this is nature's reward to offset all our sleep deprivation and all that crying!

Laughter punctuates our speech during normal conversation as we seamlessly switch back and forth between laughter and speech modes. Surprisingly, most laughter follows really innocuous lines and is not in response to jokes. We do not need our vision to laugh. The blind laugh. And we can laugh uproariously on the telephone.

Even more than smiling, laughter is a social activity, occurring 30 times more frequently in social settings. We hear so much laughter at a "good" party. It plays an important role in social bonding and cementing friendships. Is laughter, like smiling, one reason that people who socialize the most suffer the least from depression?

Kids definitely laugh more easily than older adults. Many think that one of laughter's fundamental roles is to facilitate cooperation between people. In that regard, it is intriguing to note that laughter is more common between humans who are not that closely related genetically—thus distant cousins or completely unrelated individuals laugh more together than brother and sister or parent and child. Those without shared DNA might have needed a little more incentive to help one another.

You really need to do good fieldwork to unravel some of the mysteries of laughter. And once you tell a group of people that you are observing their laughter—well, that's a show stopper that is really going to ruin your research.

Overcoming these difficulties, researchers have discovered quite a bit about laughter. Women laugh more than men, but men get more laughs. Men are also more commonly the instigators of humor. Speakers laugh more than their audiences, and laughter can be a signal of social dominance. In southern India, where the official caste system is still influential, lower caste men giggle when addressing those of a higher caste. This has also been shown among the Bahutu in Central Africa and at a Western psychiatric hospital. Laughing can sometimes be a way to show deference.

All humans develop the ability to produce and perceive laughter. It is innate and has been observed in all tribes of humans around the world. There even seems to be a laughter equivalent in rats, who utter a special vocalization when they are playing. The importance of this seemingly trivial activity is shown by the universal role for clowns in all bands of humans. There is no culture that exists without humor, and humor usually leads to laughter. One theory posits that clowns act as a buffer between disputants, deflecting blame from others onto themselves, helping to decrease the likelihood that the argument will end violently. Clowns and humor would have evolved to reduce social tensions, to inject positive feelings while minor quarrels and competition between rivals were worked out.

Human laughter probably evolved more than two million years ago, before we had language. It is thought to have ancient evolutionary roots in tickling and rough and tumble play. Human laughter is similar to the relaxed open mouth or play face seen in the great apes, who show a pant-like vocalization during tickling, chasing, and mock aggression. Darwin aptly described adult humor as "tickling of the mind." Noting that laughter and social grooming both release endogenous opiates, one theory suggests that the enjoyment derived from laughter eventually replaced the pleasure associated with social grooming in primates. Language would have eventually replaced grooming as the principal bonding device, and laughter would have helped this transition by maintaining pleasure associated with conversation.

Humans have had a couple of million years to create multiple roles for laughter. To mention a few, there is conversational laughter, nervous laughter, laughter between strangers to ease tensions, laughter to help maintain group identities, laughter to ridicule, and laughter as a social lubricant. One pervasive theme is incongruity and unexpectedness occurring in a safe context.

The multiplicity of roles probably accounts for much of the confusion in laughter theory and research. It is likely that many of the theories are partially correct—they break down when they tend to exclude other views. But like a protein that performs multiple functions in the same body, all dependent on context, laughter has been co-opted during human evolution to do several things. There are quite a few of these master proteins in our bodies. Why shouldn't laughter be able to perform different functions depending on the context and need?

CENTURIES AGO MANY of us would have been afraid to open our mouths widely, for it was not usually a pretty sight. Look at all those Renaissance portraits—no open smiles, no teeth showing. No floss and no dentists. Imagine a time when the barber who cut your hair also took care of your teeth (by pulling them). Teeth and laughter in the Renaissance were more associated with drunkenness and prostitution than happiness. Dirck van Baburen has painted a quintessential example of laughter in seventeenth-century Holland (see Figure 9.1).

I believe that poor dentition is one reason that laughter was negatively viewed by some until relatively recently. The view

Figure 9.1   The Procuress, 1622

that laughter is associated with mockery and ridicule can be seen in the origin of the word "laughingstock." In the 1500s, petty criminals were sometimes punished publicly by clamping their ankles, arms, or even necks into wooden stocks. This form of punishment was actually more serious than it sounds, and it was witnessed by the rest of the village folk. Not surprisingly, those individuals placed in public stocks were objects of derision, ridicule, laughter, and diminished social standing. When we visit a Renaissance fair today, we laugh at ourselves as we place each other in stocks for photos—but it used to be far more serious.

Unfortunately, in some quarters, this negative view of laughter still persists. I knew a fine young man who started a job as a medical assistant in a hospital but was subsequently fired because his easy laughter was seen as "unprofessional." He had a hearty, baritone laugh that travelled far down the corridors of sickness. His high spirits would lighten the load carried by those around him. Patients loved him. There were no complaints about the quality of his work. His infectious and uplifting spirits pleased everyone except the one who controlled his fate: his superior. She was deeply suspicious of all this laughter he was generating. Who was he laughing at? How dare he laugh when many others were grim, when patients were ill and dying? She had long ago concluded that a serious demeanor was the only fit one for the serious events that occur in hospitals. She never paused to question whether his laughter actually helped his patients. Laughter had no therapeutic value in her mind—so, sadly, she fired him, removing the one cheerful beacon that always shone in the hospital.

LAUGHTER IS ONE of the few things you don't mind "catching" from a fellow human. Like a domino game, we tend to laugh in turn as an epidemic sweeps through a group, creating a wave of unconscious, involuntary jocularity cascading through a landscape of people. I still remember the little mini-epidemics of laughter in my high school homeroom. Someone would do something ridiculous, like tossing an eraser, triggering hysterical laughter that completely thwarted any attempt by the teacher to instruct. And the more you were not supposed to laugh, the more you could not resist. What was the teacher supposed to do?

Contagious laughter is well described. In 1962, three teenage girls at a Tanzanian boarding school starting laughing.

Pretty soon 95 girls could not control their laughter, forcing the school's closure for two months! Who needs snow days when you can laugh? The "epidemic" spread until it forced the closing of more than 14 schools. Sounds pretty funny until you learn that it took more than a year to quell the epidemic, and that the school where it all started was sued (I can just imagine the transcript of the trial). The only successful "treatment" was a public health–style quarantine of affected laughers. This true story powerfully shows our ability and desire to imitate the behavior of one another, especially when the social stakes are high, as in adolescence.

Have you ever wondered how laughter, or for that matter any behavior, spreads among humans? To help understand why humans sometimes act like a herd of sheep in their tendency to follow one another (think about the never-ending stream of speculative bubbles), let us learn about mirror neurons.

Mirror Neurons

It was a summer day almost 20 years ago when researchers in Parma, Italy, left a monkey in a laboratory when they went out to lunch. Now this was a special monkey. He had electrodes implanted in the part of his brain responsible for planning and carrying out movements. Whenever he would pick up and move an object, the monitor, which recorded the firing of the neurons, would emit a blip of a sound. One of the graduate students had just finished lunch and entered the lab with an ice cream cone. Then the strangest thing happened. When he raised his hand to lick the ice cream, the monitor sounded as the monkey watched him eat ice cream. Initially, the graduate student couldn't believe his eyes. But the same thing happened when the researchers ate peanuts, raisins, or bananas. It had nothing whatsoever to do with what they ate but rather with the process of raising their hands to their mouths and eating. After a while they realized they had discovered a special class of neurons, called mirror neurons, that fire when we, or monkeys, hear or see an action without actually carrying it out.

These neurons allow us to do many magical things, including empathizing with others. (It also makes us realize that primates may be more aware than we want to imagine when we see them in a cage.) The human brain has many types of mirror neuron systems that allow us to carry out and understand not just actions of others, but also their intentions and emotions. We grasp the minds of others by literally feeling what they do. The contagion of laughter is just one demonstration of mirror neurons in action. By joining a party of laughter, you signal to the group your readiness to share, to cooperate.

WHY IS LAUGHTER so prevalent? What is it really doing? And why should laughter be contagious? Here is one theory that seems plausible enough though it is impossible to prove.

The life of our human ancestors millions of years ago was quite stressful. (Some things never change, only now we worry about our jobs rather than about tigers.) Then, as now, prolonged periods of stress were bad for one's health. But stress is useful when running away from tigers. It's just that prolonged emotional stress takes its toll on our bodies. Acute stress gets our hearts pounding and prepares our muscles for action, as in fighting or running. But early humans needed some way of quickly changing the mood and decreasing the stress level of the group when they had had enough food to eat and were safe from predators. Their periods of safety, times when they needed to relax, times to restore their mind and body, were brief. They needed their relaxation as much as we do. Before we could communicate with language, we signaled to others our good fortune by laughing, which promoted social cohesion and cooperation, reduced social tensions, and improved the mood of everyone around us. Laughing would cascade through the group of humans using the mirror neurons we just learned about. Laughing was a way of quickly spreading playful, happy, and healthful emotions, allowing the whole group to take advantage of a short, safe interlude. The roles of laughter in human interactions have definitely expanded in the last couple of million years, to include derision and mockery, but it is usually still a healthful behavior that tips the emotional scales in the positive direction. And laughter is usually not deceptive in nature.

I often think of the human mind as a sailboat buffeted by the winds. Let us say that in healthy living you are traveling due north at sea. A stressful event makes us angry and fearful, tenses our muscles, and raises our blood pressure, blowing us off course to the east. Our stress hormones are released to cope with the emergency. If the stress hormones persist, we feel mentally and physically drained. Prolonged stress leads to weakening of our internal organs, crippling our immune systems, weakening our bones, damaging our muscles, and impairing our memory.

When all the alarms have faded, we need to get back on course by sailing west, that is, by engaging in mirthful laughter with friends and loved ones. Laughter is a way to show the group that the sound of a rattlesnake was in fact a stick cracking, a signal of a false alarm. The positive emotion of laughter represents part of a homeostatic mechanism for our whole being and for groups of humans. As Sir William Osler, the great physician, once said, laughter is the "music of life." And Groucho Marx was on to something when he said, "A clown is like an aspirin, except it works twice as fast."

Have you ever noticed how prevalent laughter is among children and teenagers? Kids are always spontaneously playing little games with one another, laughing at the silliest things. Left to their own devices, a group of five-year-olds can transform an uneventful day into something magical. Try remembering back to a day filled with mirth and spontaneous laughter. What feelings are reactivated in your brain? Good ones. Kids are usually better at playing, having fun, and being happy. The adults are usually looking much more sullen and serious than their children. My question is, should the children really be our teachers? Picasso once said it took him quite a while to learn to paint like a child again. What is wrong with laughter and acting silly? Nothing. We need to make it much more culturally acceptable for adults to laugh, for any and for *no* reason. It is not crazy to laugh, it is wise.

It is not what happens but how we react to it that determines our mood. If you are stuck in a traffic jam, you can let yourself get angry, but who are you helping? Certainly not yourself. Most situations have a ludicrous, funny side to them, and we need to celebrate that aspect.

In the same way that we have two counterbalancing sets of muscles to hold us erect as we walk, our minds use two sets of facial muscles to balance our emotions. The yin and yang of the face. The corrugator or frown muscle takes us down the stressful path. The path of anger or fear or sadness. All of those emotions tend to draw us away from open, friendly behavior. We correct our emotional balance by smiling and laughing, creating positive feelings about one another and reducing stress hormones. Our minds and bodies continuously and unconsciously monitor our emotional balance by the process we termed earlier, *emotional proprioception*. Just as our pancreas pays attention to our eating of a sugary sweet, keeping track of our blood glucose, so too does our brain continuously and seamlessly evaluate our emotional set point. But unlike our insulin level, we have the ability to consciously affect our emotional well-being by playing, smiling, and laughing whenever we can. By using laughter, we can gain relief from the negative impact of emotions such as fear, anger, and sadness. Humor and laughter help us release the hold that negative emotions have on us, providing a way to detach ourselves from a painful event.

As far back as biblical times, humor was thought to be therapeutic: "A merry heart doeth good like a medicine: but a broken spirit drieth the bones" (Proverbs 17:22). In the thirteenth century, physicians and philosophers were writing how laughter benefited our health primarily through exercising the muscles, the lungs, and some of our inner organs. They thought that laughter enriched the blood, improved our circulation, helped with digestion, and improved our breathing.

Humor was also valued for its creation of emotional catharsis. Medieval physicians even told their patients jokes. But I don't think most physicians today employ laughter for fear that their actions might be misinterpreted. Laughter remains to this day a largely unused part of medicine that could be so powerful in its influence.

THE POSITIVE VIEW of laughter got a big boost when Norman Cousins described his experiences with laughter as the best medicine in his bestselling book *Anatomy of an Illness*. Cousins's story starts more than 50 years ago. He was young, married, and the father of four children, so he thought it prudent to get life insurance, and his aunt just happened to be an insurance agent. He felt great when he walked into the doctor's office for the physical but not so great a few days later. The life insurance company gave him a most unwelcome surprise by turning him down. The prognosis is grave, the doctor told his aunt, his heart is sick; by ceasing most of his physical activity, he might live a year and a half. They advised him to stop his frenetic life, take to his bed, and give up everything including his work, travel, and all sports.

He couldn't believe it. He was at the top of his game, whether as a rising editor at the *Saturday Review* or on the courts playing tennis several times a week. He urgently made an appointment to see the head of cardiology at Mount Sinai Hospital, expecting him to refute the findings of the insurance physical. Not so lucky. The cardiologist informed him that the electrocardiogram confirmed that he had already had a heart attack. The insurance doctors were right. And the year was 1954. There were few medications for heart disease. Terms like angioplasty, stents, and coronary artery bypass didn't yet exist.

Cousins took a deep breath. If he listened to his doctors, he had to give up everything. And what would he get for it? Maybe a year or two. The decision was easy. Cousins relates in the book, "When I came home that night, my little daughters came running to me. They liked to be thrown high in the air and to dive from my shoulders onto the couch. . . . If I accepted the advice of the specialists I would never throw my girls in the air again." He didn't tell his wife what the prophets of doom and gloom had told him, and he began playing a set or two of tennis every day! Three years later, he met a famed heart specialist who told him that he had done the only thing that could have saved his life. He wound up living to the ripe old age of 85. All his vigorous exercise actually helped strengthen his heart. But was it only exercise that kept Cousins alive? No. If he had given in to the dismal forecasts, they probably would have been self-fulfilling. His optimistic thinking empowered him to take charge of his own health. Instead of being a passive recipient of bad news, he became an active creator of good news. Cousins's mental vigor helped give his body a new lease on life.

This wasn't Cousins's first experience in coping with a grim medical diagnosis. When he was ten, a chest x-ray showed what appeared to be tuberculosis (years later he would learn that was probably a mistaken diagnosis). He spent the next six months in a sanatorium. What he noticed immediately was how the patients divided themselves into two groups: those who felt confident that they would defeat their disease, and those who resigned themselves to a serious and possibly fatal illness. He became friends with the optimistic group, who immersed themselves in creative activities. Those who resigned themselves to the worst had little to do with the optimistic group. What he found remarkable was the much higher percentage of kids from his optimistic group who left the sanatorium as cures! Conversely, those who believed in their pessimistic prophecy helped fulfill it. So even at age ten, he became aware of the power of the mind in curing disease.

Yet again, in 1964, Cousins was put to another Herculean test. He developed severe inflammatory arthritis that was greatly restricting his ability to move. His joints were so painful he was having trouble walking. Laboratory tests showed that his sedimentation rate (a blood test that is a general measure of how sick one's body is) was sky high: objective bad news. Once again he listened to a grim prognosis from his doctors. He has an incurable, debilitating arthritis that was usually fatal. The current drugs were not up to the task. His physicians thought his situation fairly hopeless.

But Cousins possessed a vitally strong will to live, coupled with a powerful ability to believe in himself. He decided he would, once again, beat the odds by doing everything in his power to lift his spirits—not *try* to beat the odds, but simply beat them. He would literally laugh his way back to good health. Groucho Marx and Alan Funt of *Candid Camera*, the TV show, became his closest friends. His family physician was open-minded enough to support his innovative therapeutic approach, empowering Cousins to take charge of his own health. He began treating himself with megadoses of laughter. The miracle began. His sedimentation rate, a marker for his disease, began to drop. He kept himself laughing in spite of all the pain. The more he laughed, the better her felt, mentally and physically. Slowly he reversed his incapacitating disease.

Years later, he told his story in an influential *New England Journal of Medicine* article. "Hearty laughter is a good way to jog internally without having to go outside," Cousins wrote. "It moves your internal organs around. It enhances respiration. It is an igniter of great expectations." Letters poured in from supportive physicians all over who recognized the power of the mind to heal the body. He then wrote *Anatomy of an Illness*, which crystalized the idea of laughter being an effective treatment—medicine—in the minds of scientists and physicians—all health care workers—as well as the general public, helping to give birth to a burgeoning "humor and health" movement (particularly in the West, as Eastern traditions have focused on this connection since ancient times).

Why did laughing help Cousins's arthritis? Or was Cousins's just a remarkable case of self-delusion? Researchers in Japan asked the question directly. Can laughing actually affect your levels of a hormone in your blood known to be associated with arthritis?

They had rheumatoid arthritis patients and healthy controls watch an hour performance of a "Rakugo," a traditional Japanese comic story. They were trying to see whether the serum hormone interleukin-6 (IL6), which has been shown to be associated with joint pain and swelling, would lower in the arthritis suffers when exposed to "mirthful" (as in truly emotional) laughter. It definitely did, and levels of the stress hormone cortisol also dropped. Shortly afterward their findings were supported when a monoclonal antibody that attacks IL-6 was shown to be significantly effective in treating rheumatoid arthritis. I'm sure that Norman Cousins would be smiling now. Somehow that seemingly meaningless activity of laughter lowered the level of a damaging hormone in our blood.

How could laughter actually reduce stress? Normal subjects who watched a funny one-hour video had lower levels of the hormones that tear down our tissues and raise our blood pressure. All of these hormones are part of the body's classic response to stress, thus showing biochemical ways that laughter can help reverse stress, improving our physical energy, mood, and sense of well-being.

Another group of scientists asked whether certain antibodies that protect us from infections could be elevated by laughter. The researchers measured antibody levels in healthy subjects before and after they watched both a 75-minute comic film and, on a different day, an unemotional control film. They quantified laughter by electrically determining how much their subjects' smile muscles were contracting.

They found that an important antibody that helps protect the nose and throat from colds and other viruses increased dramatically after the subjects watched a humorous video, while it didn't change after they watched a video that was emotionally neutral. These and other studies show that laughter directly benefits our immune system, along with reducing our level of stress hormones, and suggest how it might well improve one's health. So the next time you feel yourself coming down with a cold, perhaps it is not so flippant after all to suggest that you go rent a funny movie and start laughing.

The field of laughter research is in its infancy—we do not know what is happening in our brains after we laugh, nor do we know much about how laughter affects our bodies. Only more research can firmly place laughter on solid footing as a therapeutic modality.

THE MOVEMENT TO popularize laughter as a healthful treatment got a big push in 1995 when Dr. Madan Kataria, a Mumbai physician, discovered the physical and psychological benefits enjoyed by his patients who had taken to heart his prescription for regular laughter. They were happier, healthier, and more productive. Dr. Kataria was really concerned about the effect of stress on people who lived in Mumbai (formerly called Bombay), India's most populous city and one of the most populous in the world, with an estimated population in 2006 of about 13 million. With a density of about 18,000 people per square mile, city life there is definitely stressful. So one day Dr. Kataria went out into a park and asked as many people as he could to join him in an instant laughter club. Eventually he managed to persuade four people to join him. As others watched in initial bemusement, they took it in turns to tell jokes. We have seen how infectious laughter is. Others started to join, and soon he had 50 people in his club.

Unfortunately, they ran out of jokes after two weeks, and then some complained because the humor had become sexist and rude. To rescue his new idea—and this was the crucial breakthrough—Dr. Kataria turned to the idea of laughter exercises to help people fake laughter, which worked really well.

He also turned to his wife, a yoga teacher, and incorporated yoga's deep-breathing practice, which he adapted to simple breathing exercises to support people's ability to sustain the laughter beneficially. Laughter (Hasya) Yoga was born, his club recovered, and soon the park was attracting large numbers to pre-work laughter sessions. It proved so popular that it spread all around India.

Laughter clubs have subsequently formed all over the world. People of all ages, religions, and ethnicities laugh together, laughing as they have never laughed before, leaving refreshed and invigorated. It is a communal activity aimed at promoting health and well-being. But laughter remains, to this day, an under-recognized well from which to draw health and happiness. Maybe we should listen to e. e. cummings, who said, "The most wasted of all days is one without laughter."

CHAPTER 10

PESSIMISM, DEPRESSION, AND OPTIMISM

"For as he thinketh in his heart, so is he."

—Proverbs 23:7

DEPRESSION HAS BEEN seen in man for countless generations. Of what use is a state that robs one of all pleasure, makes one irritable, impairs normal activities, and can be deadly? Many psychologists believe that depression often starts from pessimism gone awry. In the cognitive model of learned helplessness and depression, thinking pessimistic, sad thoughts actually helps cause and sustain the depression. If you feel powerless to control unfortunate events unfolding around you, the helpless feeling, whether valid or not, can precipitate a depression. It's not that you become depressed and therefore think sad thoughts; rather the pessimism actually causes the depression.

If you blame yourself for bad events, then your self-criticism, rather than the negative event itself, may make you sad. Thus, psychologists help their patients by re-tinting the lenses through which they view the world.

When pessimism colors one's views of oneself, depression often ensues. Altering pessimistic thoughts about oneself is part of cognitive therapy, which emphasizes positive self-evaluation and more realistic explanations of outcomes around you.

Now if pessimism is so potentially destructive to one's emotional health, why have it? What is the evolutionary reason for us to be pessimistic some of the time?

Pessimism has its origins in reality. Researchers have shown that pessimists tend to predict dangerous outcomes better than optimists. A pessimist evaluates risks carefully, which may improve survival under adverse circumstances.

I think of my grandfather, Seidel, working in a factory with no ventilation, in New York in 1910. He was a fun-loving, handsome, and carefree fellow who, however, was quite a realist when it came to sizing up the odds. He had to be to survive. He was only 11, and the oldest child, when his father fell from a roof while building a house in Russia. Life took a dark turn when his family fended for themselves after his father's death. In the dead of night, he would climb over tall fences to sneak into slaughterhouses to steal meat for his starving family. He reckoned that life had to be better in America, so a few years later he and his brother emigrated to the United States.

He played the piano, the violin, and the mandolin, but it would be years before he fully supported himself from his music. He worked alongside his brother until his brother started coughing incessantly. Soon it became clear that his cough was worsening, a sure sign of tuberculosis. At the turn of the century, before the discovery of antibiotics, Seidel could do little but watch his brother slowly waste away. He might have thought that somehow he was stronger than his younger brother and would resist catching the dreaded consumption. Instead, he reasoned that he was less likely to die from tuberculosis if he worked outdoors in the fresh air. He had already seen others who worked indoors succumb to the disease. He was correct in his realistic assessment of tuberculosis—indoor work meant more exposure to infectious air. So he got a job painting bridges hundreds of feet in the air. He knew he could walk the steel beams. For him the heights weren't risky. He told me he felt comfortable way up high, completing the work at his own pace, far away from the scrutiny of his boss. The heights didn't scare him, but tuberculosis did. His sober realism paid off. He survived.

Six years later the world was embroiled in a war in Europe that claimed thousands of lives in a single battle. My grandfather read the newspapers like everyone else and knew about the horrendous conditions under which the soldiers fought. Those who survived the bullets often died from disease caught in the cold, wet trenches. He reckoned it was only a matter of time before America entered the war. He had experienced enough cold for a lifetime in Russia. When he heard about a Canadian regiment that was going to be sent to Palestine, he reckoned that the warm Middle East would be safer than the cold muddy trenches, so he volunteered to become a Canadian Royal Fusilier. He looked a lot happier in pictures from the Middle

East than he would have been in the mud. Aside from falling ill with malaria, he survived the war without injury. Again, his pessimistic but realistic evaluation of World War I turned out to be correct. He never became depressed because he never viewed *himself* pessimistically. Eventually he lived to fulfill his lifelong dream of immersing himself in music.

Learned Helplessness

In the 1970s, Martin Seligman and others helped to develop the learned helplessness model of depression. This influential theory predicts that the individual will be prone to depression when she/he no longer feels in control of her/his destiny, when she/he feels helpless in the face of adversity. By working with this model, clinical psychologists have made good progress in the treatment of depression.

Darwin is prescient when he states, "If we expect to suffer, we are anxious; if we have no hope of relief, we despair."

I gained some insight into my mother's depression by revisiting her childhood. When the Great Depression hit, all those odd jobs my grandfather had playing the piano at a club or the mandolin at a restaurant just disappeared. My mother was only four years old when the family fortunes hit bottom. Facing eviction, her father felt completely inadequate in his role as family provider. His musical skills were not in demand during the Great Depression. He tried to convince his wife to go to one of the private welfare agencies, but she stubbornly refused. So he said, "If I leave you, then you will have to go for help, and with your husband gone, they will have to give you money for rent and food. I will try and find work outside of New York and return when I've saved some money." While my grandfather Seidel was right about the physical help that the welfare agency would provide, he never realized the psychological devastation his leaving would cause.

One day my mother's world lost an important half when her father left to look for work. He didn't write. He just disappeared. I don't think he realized how cruel he was by not writing. Years earlier he had begun to spin an emotional cocoon around his feelings to protect himself from the loss of his father. The cocoon hardened with the death of his brother and the loss of his mother and siblings, whom he was destined never to see again. His way of dealing with loss was not to deal with it at all—he just went on with his life and avoided thinking about the troublesome details. Not writing may have helped him to cope with another loss, in this case, the loss of work and family, but it was tragic for his wife, Rosie, and my mother, Hilda. He may have thought he was actually helping his family in the long run by looking for work and saving money for them. But my grandmother Rosie had no idea if or when he might return. She cried as weeks passed into months. Still no word from Seidel. Rosie's temperament was diametrically opposed to Seidel's. She worried constantly while overprotecting my mother as much as he had underprotected her.

My mother, Hilda, remembered chilling thoughts that would overcome her in the midst of play: *Your father is dead, and you will never see his handsome face or hear his music again.* She had no idea that he rode the freight trains out west, working on farms, getting odd jobs here and there, exploring the country in ways he had never imagined when he moved to New York City.

My mother was devastated. Chilling thoughts would overcome her: Her aunt Sophie added to the pain by telling her sister that, "He'll never come back to you," and gloried in my grandmother's misery.

This was my mother's first taste of complete helplessness, buffeted about by directionless storms. Her pessimistic thoughts turned into a childhood depression. Then as now, economic grief translates into emotional grief as the loss of work destabilizes families trying to cope with adversity that is outside their control.

Many months later, as she walked with her mother on East Broadway, my mother spied a familiar tall, fair, lean figure coming toward them. "Mama," she cried, "there's Daddy!" Then he was with them, and she was swinging along between them, jumping for joy while they each held her hand. Her world was temporarily restored. Her father had managed to save a little money and return home unscathed. But the seeds of helplessness had been planted and would grow, years later, into a depression.

IT'S FUN TO hang around optimists. They are exciting, adventuresome, confident, and usually more willing to take risks. John F. Kennedy, Jr. was a popular, handsome optimist. But optimists take more chances since they are more convinced of their abilities. A pessimist would rather sleep in an airport than fly away with family on a foggy, rainy night, knowing that he was still learning instrument flying. The pessimist would have been tired, but the optimist John F. Kennedy, Jr. did not survive his flight into the black New England night.

Pessimists tend to do better in dangerous times, like war or flying in bad weather. But as the next study shows, most of the time it pays to be an optimist.

Can you predict disease based on the explanatory style of someone—whether they are pessimistic or optimistic? Researchers analyzed the writings of a group of Harvard freshmen who were followed longitudinally for 50 years as part of a research study started in the 1930s. These 200 men were picked from five Harvard classes for their physical and intellectual fitness. Researchers categorized the essays of these men after they returned from service in the Second World War. Based on the men's writings, they were able to divide them into pessimists or optimists. They then looked at how these men had fared in life over the years. In particular, they wanted to know how their health correlated with their outlook on life. They found that health at age 60 was strongly correlated to the optimism they showed at age 25. Pessimistic men developed chronic diseases more severely and earlier. Studies such as these have convinced me that how you view the world around you is every bit as important, if not more important, than what really happens to you.

THE DESTRUCTIVE POWER of depression is assumed by many to be solely due to its ability to deny enjoyment to its sufferers, to rob them of hope, desire, and the will to live. But the mind's power extends far beyond its physical limits, far beyond the brain's traditional functions. The brain and the body are inseparable, but Western medicine has been slow to recognize just how dependent one's physical health is on one's mental health. There are many unseen connections between our minds and our other organs.

We now have strong evidence that the mind can profoundly affect our hearts, our immune systems, and our overall health. People who suffer from depression suffer from more than just their psychic pain. Depression is a major risk factor for death. Those who are happy live an average of eight years longer than those who suffer from chronic depression. Patients with severe depression have a fourfold increased risk of having a heart attack. And those who suffer from depression are more likely to die from heart disease in the first few months after an initial heart attack. Staying happy is of more importance than its immediate hedonic effects. Smiling and laughing may actually ward off disease.

There is no shortage of stories of how the death of a loved one was followed quickly by that of their spouse or parent. Thinking terrible thoughts may actually cause one's demise. I am reminded of the sad story of how Gustave Courbet, the famous nineteenth-century French realist painter, lost his mother.

Courbet, like most of his artistic contemporaries, was supportive of the popular rebellion that swept Paris after France's humiliating defeat by Prussia in the 1871 war. Courbet was appointed minister of culture by the new and short-lived communard government. A few months later, the monarchy recaptured Paris, brutally suppressing the grass-roots rebellion and executing over 20,000 Parisians who had participated in the revolt. Rumors spread quickly, including the fateful one about the violent death of Courbet at the hands of the army. When Madame Courbet heard the rumor that evening, she refused to listen to her husband, who implored her not to lose hope until there was proof that their son was dead. (He had, in fact, fled his studio when the army reentered Paris and was later jailed and disgraced but not injured.)

Courbet's father wrote of the tragedy to his good friend Édouard Ordinaire:

> I write first to inform you that yesterday,—at three o'clock in the morning—my beloved wife left us forever. O what a loss this is..., this good mother, with a sensibility too extreme, —when she heard that her beloved son was no more?—in spite of our doing all we could to make her understand that all the stories in this respect were not justified, it is a thing that she was not able to get over in her mind.

Why would Madame Courbet die that morning? Just a coincidence or something more? We now know that the body can rapidly release stress hormones such as adrenaline after severe emotional stress. These hormones are released into our bloodstream in response to emotionally traumatic events. They are part of our "fight or flight" response, which prepares our bodies for intense physical activity by increasing blood pressure and heart rate. These neurohormones, as they're known because they affect our nervous system, acutely stress the heart, sometimes causing our hearts to beat too quickly, too irregularly, and, finally, not at all. These hormones are meant to make your heart pound faster and stronger so you can escape that tiger when you are running away. Only this tiger was in the mind of Madame Courbet, and her inability to escape from it probably led to her demise.

Doctors at Johns Hopkins have recently validated what many a poet has written about, as they have shown that a severe emotional shock can actually cause reversible heart failure, which they fittingly enough term "broken heart syndrome." Some of their patients had up to 34 times the normal level of stress hormones, which literally stun the heart, causing chest pain, shortness of breath, and fluid in the lungs. What is remarkable is that perfectly healthy young people can be so stricken when the emotions go awry.

Dr. Roy Ziegelstein, a pioneer cardiologist at Johns Hopkins, has been making connections between a person's emotions and heart function for the past 15 years. But the idea that depression itself might be one of the primary causes of heart disease is still controversial. Although it is now accepted that up to 30 percent of patients recovering from a heart attack suffer from depression, many physicians resist the conclusion that depression may have been a cause and not a consequence of heart disease.

Despite the publication of good studies documenting this connection, Ziegelstein says he has known too many perfectly smart cardiologists who say things like "stress is overrated" as a driving factor in heart disease. His message to cardiologists is clear. "If you don't attend to the patient's depression, you're really only half a doctor, in my view. And half a doctor is as good as no doctor."

Research has shown that lowering the amount of psychological distress in heart attack survivors had a direct effect on whether

they'd have another one. Scientists found that depressed sufferers of coronary disease have greater physical limitations, a worse
quality of life, and poorer overall health than subjects with heart
disease who were not depressed.

Unfortunately, doctors and nurses have proved to be poor at
recognizing symptoms of depression in patients recovering from
a heart attack. Without formal screening tests, providers missed
three out of four depressed patients. Unlike blood pressure, it is
hard to put a number on depression. Scientific advance is built
on measurement. If you can't measure something objectively
with a machine, it's hard to do experiments. But how do you
quantify pain in the brain? In the end, only the words of the
patient can tell you how happy or sad they feel. Until we devise
an objective, quantitative test for depression, one that does not
rely on words from our patients, we will have trouble convincing others of the reality of depression. Without knowing about
glucose and insulin, could we "understand" diabetes? Everyone
is sympathetic if you show up to work with your arm in a cast,
but how do you see the cast around your mind as you heal from
the loss of a loved one?

We also need to be mindful that there may be more deep-
seated explanations for health care providers' failure to deal well
with mental health issues. Perhaps it occurs because of the trivi-
alization of mental illness in society as a whole. Mental illness is
seen as a weakness, but kidney disease, heart disease, and broken
bones are not. Is it because, until recently, we did not have good
treatment for mental illness? Or might it be our fear of insanity?
A family history of insanity is like a sword of Damocles, waiting
to strike, seemingly wantonly and with vengeful power. I have

often encountered remarkable resistance in the health provider community whenever the issue of depression arises. I remember a nurse confiding to me about a patient who had sunk into a deep black hole of a mood, "Why can't she just get over it?" But I have never heard anyone criticize a diabetic patient for her unwillingness to make her pancreas produce more insulin. Somehow the brain is not accorded the same sympathy as other organs.

RESEARCHERS HAVE SHOWN that our immune systems are greatly weakened by depression, to the extent that our risk of cancer increases markedly. Our immune systems are normally on constant guard, protecting us from cells that transform into cancer. Mistakes happen all the time in our bodies, but usually our immune cells come to the rescue by halting the growth of abnormal cells that look foreign to our bodies.

There is an intricate system of checks and balances that keeps normal cell growth humming along like a finely tuned car. Our bodies truly go through birth, life, and death every single day as they make billions of new cells in the blood, gut, and skin. Yet the abnormal growth of one of those cells to form a tumor that you or I can see and feel is a rare event. When our immune systems stop working well, as when a spouse of 50 years dies, our risk of death from infection or cancer rises dramatically.

The strong interplay between the different organs provides a means for explaining why thoughts and emotions influence our bodies and vice versa. The nervous system is connected to the immune system. If our minds are suffering, our lymphocytes may suffer as well. The question is, can a complete disgrace, dishonor, or loss of our sense of self-worth do something similar to our immune systems? Can the loss of honor cause the mind to impair our lymphocytes' ability to fight cancer? It's hard to do a scientific study about disgrace, so let us revisit the story of one famous British prime minister who suffered a severe loss in social standing.

Most would agree that World War II was a horrific conflict. What would it feel like to be the head of your country and be forced to resign in utter disgrace in front of your nation? To be the one who told a nation that he could avoid a general war in return for concessions "that we don't really care about"? In 1938, Hitler had been demanding that the Sudetenland region of Czechoslovakia be annexed to Germany. After meeting with Hitler to try and negotiate his way out of the crisis, Neville Chamberlain addressed the nation by radio on a September evening and, after thanking those who wrote to him, stated:

> How horrible, fantastic, incredible it is that we should be digging trenches and trying on gas-masks here because of a quarrel in a far-away country between people of whom we know nothing. It seems still more impossible that a quarrel that has already been settled in principle should be the subject of war.

Three days later, after signing the Munich agreement in which he ceded part of Czechoslovakia to Adolf Hitler, Chamberlin stood outside 10 Downing Street while reading from the document to the crowd before him:

> My good friends, for the second time in our history, a British Prime Minister has returned from Germany bringing peace

with honor. I believe it is peace for our time. We thank you from the bottom of our hearts. Now I recommend you go home, and sleep quietly in your beds.

And the crowd cheered him. In March, Hitler invaded and seized the rest of Czechoslovakia. Chamberlain's vision of peace became a mirage. Six months later, Nazi Germany invaded Poland. Neville Chamberlain continued his appeasement policy to the bitter end, when he announced that if Hitler would withdraw his troops within two days, Britain would open talks between Germany and Poland. The outcry against Chamberlain from the British Parliament was swift, and he was forced to declare war on Germany on September 1939. That afternoon Chamberlain addressed the British House of Commons:

Everything that I have worked for, everything that I have hoped for, everything that I have believed in during my public life has crashed into ruins.

On May 7, 1940, Leo Amery, a member of Parliament who had been a personal friend of Chamberlain's, concluded his speech in the British House of Commons by quoting the words that Oliver Cromwell had said in Parliament centuries before:

You have sat too long here for any good you have been doing. Depart, I say, and let us have done with you. In the name of God, go!

On May 10, 1940, Neville Chamberlain was forced to resign. Imagine how he felt. He considered himself an honorable man, and his pursuit of peace through appeasement had been popular with many in Britain. He remembered the devastating loss of life in World War I, the killing of a whole generation of Britain's best in mud trenches. Chamberlain had sought to avoid war at all costs. He was now forced to undergo a radical reevaluation of himself and his failed policies. The shame and guilt must have been unbearable. We now know how powerfully connected the mind and body are. How our immune system is intimately linked to our thoughts and feelings. If Chamberlain had been a rogue, a psychopathic dictator without guilt or remorse, I doubt his health would have been affected. (Have you noticed how tyrants don't often die of cancer?) He had meant well but knew that history would judge him harshly. What would become of him?

In July 1940, Neville Chamberlain was diagnosed with stomach cancer, and by November 1940 he was dead. While this could all be one great coincidence, history repeats itself with those who suffer terrible shame or guilt, those who feel responsible for terrible losses. Could it be that his immune system was keeping a tumor at bay until his utter disgrace impaired his lymphocytes and allowed his cancer to grow like wildfire? We will never know for sure, but the power of our thoughts is not to be ignored.

As WE HAVE seen, we are marvelously interwoven beings, receiving inputs from hidden sources that influence all aspects of our functioning, our behavior, and our health. Our thoughts and emotions are connected to our stress hormones as we try to balance risk and danger with pleasure. How do our faces interface with the cycle of emotions and stress (see Figure 10.1)?

Let us start at the top of this simplified cycle with happiness, good health, and decreased chronic disease. If you are happy, you have lower levels of stress hormones in your system and less risk of suffering from a chronic disease. Your body is undergoing less wear and tear because it is relaxed and calm. If sad thoughts, negative emotions (such as anger, sadness, and fear), and frowning increase and become persistent, you become more pessimistic, and more stress hormones are released into your bloodstream. The stress hormones are meant to help you cope with an emergency situation, like a famine, war, or imminent danger. But if this situation continues, as in divorce, chronic illness, or unemployment, it may ultimately lead to the bottom of the cycle, where depression takes over and chronic diseases

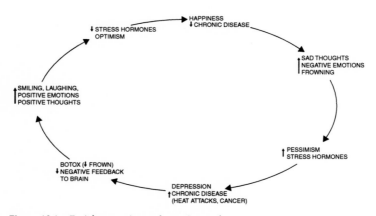

Figure 10.1   Facial expression and emotion cycle

become even more prevalent. Botulinum toxin can help interrupt this cycle, with decreased negative feedback to the brain. And if you smile and laugh more, and have more positive thoughts, this is self-reinforcing and leads to optimism and lower levels of stress hormones, along with a reduced likelihood of debilitating, chronic disease. And feeling healthier and stronger can hopefully help you remain at the top of the cycle, where you are happy. At any entrance point to the cycle, positive thoughts, emotions, and facial expressions will help steer you in the right direction. Although our functioning is much more complex than what is shown, I do believe that the basic principles apply.

CHAPTER 11

NON-COSMETIC COSMETIC SURGERY

"Sometimes your joy is the source of your smile, but sometimes your smile can be the source of your joy."

—Thich Nhat Hanh

THERE IS SOMETHING I call non-cosmetic cosmetic surgery. This is the ultimate oxymoron, except that it really does make sense. Suppose your face conveys to the world around you an impression that differs greatly from the way you really feel. I would argue that correction of that is not really cosmetic but rather necessary to synchronize your outside with your inside. All of us would recognize that repair of a cleft lip is not cosmetic in nature—you can't look at a poor child with this deformity without having sympathy—yet I'm not sure how many of us would recognize that an angry expression that has no anger behind it could be a huge problem.

Most of the time our faces display and project to others what we are feeling inside, whether we are consciously aware of it or not. But occasionally our faces project to the outside world emotions that don't exist inside. What happens when our faces communicate the wrong message?

Look the Way You Feel

When I walked into the exam room, I couldn't help but notice Paul D.'s face, full of vigor and health except for his frown. Paul had a pleasant manner and seemed quite at ease. But his face showed a strong and constant furrow between his eyebrows. When I asked him what had brought him to my office, he answered, "Well, I feel fine, but my wife always asks me if I'm mad with her or upset about something. I try to reassure her, but it never seems to work. So I thought that you might be able to get rid of the lines that are bothering her." Taking a close look at Paul, I realized that he was really disconnected from the face he wore. His brow looked upset and troubled, with deep angry lines running down between his eyebrows, all quite out of place with Paul's peaceful demeanor. I treated him with Botox, which relaxed his frown.

Two months later, Paul told me that life was now so much easier at home because his wife no longer worried about him all the time. He could look in the mirror and think, "Well, now at least I look how I feel."

Reverse Smiley

I first met Amy L. when she came to my office because of a changing mole. Her father had suffered several bouts with mela-noma, so she was understandably concerned when one of her moles started growing. Her reddish hair and hazel eyes also put her at higher risk for skin cancer. Fortunately, the mole I removed from her chest turned out to be normal.

When she came back in for follow-up, she confided in me that she was not totally happy with her face. Amy was an attractive woman in her early forties. Her skin was healthy and clear. I asked what was bothering her. She pointed to the corners of her mouth and said, "They look sad!" Her face was young looking, but she wore a slight but consistent mouth frown unless she was actively smiling. She complained, "Unless I smile all the time, people get the wrong idea. They think I'm a little bit upset, sometimes with them."

A reverse smiley. It was subtle, but our minds are so good at picking up the nuances of facial expressions.

As we age, most of us lose fat and bone around the mouth. The net effect is a downward pointing of the corners of the mouth. Amy and I talked about the treatment options, and she decided to have me put a synthetic filler into the corners of her mouth that day. (Fillers are usually chemically related to real components of the skin—only they are made in the laboratory. They mimic fat or collagen under the skin.) The filler lifted the corners of her mouth so that they no longer pointed down at rest. Thanks to this tissue support, within minutes she could look in the mirror and see that her sad look was gone.

Can Frowning Ruin Your Marriage?

I certainly never seriously considered that thought until one of my patients, Jane L., told me her story. Unlike Paul and

Amy, when Jane frowned, she really meant it. Jane was a tall, strongly built, attractive woman in her late thirties. When she first came to see me, she had a somewhat masculine figure, with more weight around her abdomen and waist than she would like. For as long as we have had records, men have preferred women with hips that are larger than their waists. The ideal waist-to-hip ratio for a woman in terms of attractiveness is around 0.7. Women with such diverse figures as Audrey Hepburn, Sophia Loren, and Twiggy have all had ratios close to 0.7. Men probably find this type of figure appealing because it usually signals an optimal level of estrogen and is associated with good health and higher fertility. Conversely, women prefer tall men with V-shaped upper torsos and waist-to-hip ratios of 0.9, as this signals good health along with increased strength and fertility.

Jane had been a really good athlete in high school and college and had a stronger upper body than most women. She asked me to make her figure more feminine by performing liposuction. She also had beautiful, light brown, unblemished skin that registered her every facial expression extremely clearly. She frowned easily and frequently during the course of our conversation. She seemed to have an unusually animated corrugator muscle whose movement punctuated innocent exchanges during the course of a conversation, even though the rest of her face was not more expressive than usual.

Jane told me that the strong frown lines between her brows bothered her. She asked whether I could help soften them as they did not fit with the rest of her face. I injected Botox into her frown muscles. I saw her again in six weeks for follow-up, and everything was fine. I lost touch with her until two years later, when she returned to discuss removing fat from her arms. Her torso looked great, thanks to a good fitness regimen, but she wanted to slim down her arms. As I looked through her chart, I saw that she had come to our office faithfully, every three months, to have Botox injections for her frown lines by one of my associates. I asked how the Botox was working for her.

Jane said, "I used to have all these fights with my man. He would do something to annoy me, and I would frown. I didn't even know it was happening. Then he would ask me if I was mad with him. I tried to deny it, but my face couldn't lie. So he would start to argue, and it went downhill from there.

"Now I get a little annoyed with him now and then, but my face doesn't show it. He'll ask me, 'Are you mad, babe?' And I'll say no, and he believes me! And even if I was angry, it all calms down quickly, so I really am much happier with him! We no longer fight like we used to. We get along so much better."

She felt less angry, at least in part, because of her inability to frown. Her frown had played the role of pouring kerosene on a smoldering fire. It stimulated a self- reinforcing feedback loop of negative emotions that strained her relationship with her husband. Breaking that feedback loop kept her marriage on more positive ground.

Facial expressions are definitely contagious. We all recognize how laughter can spread, but the same applies for the negative emotions. Over 2,000 years ago, the Roman poet Ovid recognized this when he wrote, "A new idea is delicate. It can be killed by a sneer or a yawn; it can be stabbed to death by a quip and worried to death by a frown on the right man's brow."

The Ravages of a Successful Diet

Timothy P. was a vigorous 74-year-old military veteran who told me how he once shot a moose with a revolver! The kind of gentleman I would want as my platoon leader if I were a foot soldier in a war, the kind of man General Patton would have wanted in his army. He said, "Hey, Doc, I guess you don't do a whole lot of shooting," as he looked at my paintings adorning the walls of the exam room. "You must be busy with your painting." He smiled when I told him how I used to enjoy shooting pennies with a 22 when I was a kid. He opened up more and said, "Now, Doc, I've got a problem. When I go out to eat, the waitress looks at me funny and asks why I'm so angry with her."

Timothy was a happy fellow who enjoyed life. He loved socializing and going out to eat. Although his wife had died a few years before, he managed to remain upbeat. But his mouth turned so far down that he really did look as if he were frowning. He was telling the truth when he said he was happy, but his hangdog look caused a visceral angst within me and many others. The waitress was unusual for verbalizing what everyone else was feeling.

Even though I knew better, I felt that Timothy's face was expressing displeasure with me. My conscious mind had trouble suppressing the message that my unconscious kept telling it. Timothy looked angry, and my rational, cognitive mind could not suppress the opinion of the evolutionarily older parts of my brain that produced the sort of gut reactions we all experience. His frown caused me anxiety, as my unconscious brain insisted that this frown represented possible danger.

"So, Doc, do think you can help me?" I looked at Timothy's face and realized it was all the extra skin that was pulling his mouth down. He had lost a hundred pounds, which was great for his health but bad for his face. The skin becomes less elastic as we age, and rather than tightening as he lost fat, Timothy's facial skin now drooped far down on both sides, creating a strong mouth frown. No matter how hard he tried to smile, the sea of extra skin defeated him.

Here was a man who really deserved help, I thought to myself. His face was ruining his life by projecting an unhappy disposition to the world around him.

"Timothy, I think we can really help you by lifting up all the extra skin so that your face appears more neutral to others."

A week after the surgery to pull up the lower part of his face and mouth, Timothy came in for his follow-up appointment.

"How are you doing?" I asked.

"Not too bad, Doc; was only a little sore on one side for a few days."

I felt more at ease with him immediately because of the way he looked. What amazed me was how much better I felt around him. He had not changed in personality, but my unconscious feelings toward him had changed dramatically. It was remarkable how a simple change of the shape of someone's mouth could influence me even though I was the one who performed the change. Our brain's program to respond to facial expressions is so innate, and so powerful, that we are unable to resist its pull in spite of what we may know consciously.

Of course, Timothy had wanted to change everyone's reaction to him, not just mine. So it was great to hear him say, "My son says I look a lot happier." His friends said the same, and waitresses and others he met day to day no longer assumed he was mad. Now he could eat a nice restaurant meal without having to explain why looked but did not feel angry.

CHAPTER 12

FUTURE DIRECTIONS

"A man will be imprisoned in a room with a door that's unlocked and opens inwards; as long as it does not occur to him to pull rather than push."

—Ludwig Wittgenstein

WHERE DO WE go from here? How can we use our current knowledge about botulinum toxin and human emotions to predict future areas of research?

We are at the beginning of a new way of influencing emotions and moods, using facial muscles to gain access to the brain. There are many more questions than answers. We do not know who will respond best to botulinum toxin or how wide its applicability to mental health will eventually become. Does it help bipolar depressed patients? Do men respond as well as women? How well does it help those with profound depression? Is there any correlation between frown muscle activity (as determined electrically) and response to botulinum toxin?

To find answers to these questions, we need to learn more about how muscles feed back to the brain. What actually happens in the brain when the frown muscle is inactive? How do these changes relate to the changes induced by current antidepressant medications? Can you see changes in neurotransmitters after inactivating frown muscles? What about other mental health problems unrelated to depression?

Here is the story of one of my patients who used botulinum toxin to help control his anger.

Phil was a likeable, soft-spoken, Midwestern-born transplant to the Washington, DC, area. He came to my office seeking treatment for a small skin cancer near his right eye. His fair skin and blue eyes were no match for southern sunshine. We spoke about removing the cancer by a special technique called Mohs surgery, named for an indefatigable surgeon named Frederic Mohs, another Midwesterner. Dr. Mohs had spent the better part of his long life traveling around the country teaching his special technique to newfound converts, mostly dermatologists. Before Dr. Mohs came along, skin cancer tissue was removed by a surgeon and then examined by a pathologist who sectioned the tissue the same way you slice a loaf of bread. But the pathologist only looks at the edges, or faces of the slices, not what is inside. Because there is a lot of bread in each slice, conventional surgery has difficulty curing certain types of skin cancers, particularly facial ones, as it may miss some remaining cancer cells that are contained in the tissue but not visible on the parts of the tissue examined by the pathologist.

Fred Mohs figured out that thin horizontal rather than vertical sections could allow one to directly visualize microscopically the entire boundaries of the tumor. This led to much higher cure rates. It also allowed one to literally map out the tumor, how it grew in three dimensions, thus enabling the surgeon to remove only tissue that contained a tumor. The patient was thus spared the wholesale and potentially disfiguring removal of normal tissue.

It's a shame they don't give posthumous Nobel Prizes. Fred Mohs would deserve one. But Dr. Mohs was one of those self-effacing types who just wanted to help cure people of their cancer. He never made a dime from his discovery. For all those patients, including Phil, who have had their skin cancers successfully removed without cosmetic disfigurement, I raise my glass to Dr. Mohs. It is remarkable just how simple his idea is. Dr. Mohs was embraced by dermatologists, who accepted him and his technique, modifying it so it could become the practical office procedure frequently performed today. His tireless teaching convinced a generation of dermatologists that Mohs surgery was the gold standard against which all other treatments for skin cancer should be compared.

Sometime after I had removed Phil's cancer by Mohs surgery, he returned to my office to discuss a different matter. He was bipolar but very stable on his medication. He was, however, coping with another big issue. He had a somewhat irritable temperament and was easily angered. Phil was helping to raise his wife's kids from her first marriage, and he sometimes lost his cool with his stepchildren. He was a perfectionist, but his wife's children were almost teenagers when he entered the household, so he became frustrated with habits that were so unlike his own and difficult to change. He was orderly and organized and couldn't stand to see the chaos that his stepchildren generated. His temper definitely did not help endear him to his kids or his wife. So he asked me, "Do you think that Botox could help me become less irritable?" Phil had a sister who worked in the mental health field and had heard of Botox helping depression, so she sent her brother to ask me whether it might help him control his temper. Phil was not depressed, so I told him that I really didn't know if it would help, but that it would be worth a try. The hope was that his inability to contract his corrugator muscle, the contraction of which is associated with anger, might help dampen his anger and irritability.

Phil had pretty powerful frown muscles, so we tried botulinum toxin. I saw him again two weeks later. He really hadn't expected to see any difference. He was skeptical that such a simple treatment could actually affect something as complex as his temper and irritability.

"I seem to be less prone to get upset over the things the kids do (or more often, don't do)," he told me. "I don't really understand how this is working, but my wife says keep it up."

Phil comes back periodically for his botulinum toxin treatments, and for several years now, he has felt in better control of his temper. Of course, one case doesn't prove much, but I hope researchers will do studies to test whether botulinum toxin can help control anger. There aren't any magic bullets for anger, so any tool that could help blunt anger without significant side effects would be a welcome addition to our medical toolbox.

For now, let us suppose that botulinum toxin does work in many patients to dampen anger. What kinds of paths would that information lead us down? What other aspects of our health could it help us with?

It turns out that there is a pretty strong association betwee-namong anger, hostility, and heart disease. Angry people have lots of bad-for-you hormones circulating in their blood as their bodies remain in a perpetual state of readiness for a fight with a guy sitting on the next bar stool. While those hormones might help win a fight, most of us don't need to brawl on a daily basis, so those hormones we inherited from our ancestors are not useful most of the time. Not only are they not useful, they are downright dangerous. If you're ready to punch out the next guy, you're actually attacking your own body at the same time. The turbulence that anger can engender exists within your body as well as your mind. You clot more easily and have higher levels of inflammatory molecules in your blood waiting to help repair that wound after the fight. All this inflammation is not good for your blood vessels—they can plug up more easily. Because your heart is nourished every second of the day by those blood vessels, a clot can cause a heart attack.

Sixty-five years ago, a couple of cardiologists were redoing their office decor when they noticed that the fabric on the chairs was not wearing normally. You might expect that the whole seat of the chair would gradually wear out as people of all different shapes and sizes sat down. The center of the chair should be most worn, with a gradual decrease around the periphery. Over time the random fluctuations in sitting should result in a sym-metric pattern of wear. But that is not what the cardiologists found. Their patients wore out the fabric in a peculiar pattern. The fronts of the chairs were much more worn. Their heart disease patients were more often than not sitting and leaning forward. As part of their disease, they had more trouble relaxing. They were ready to bolt up out of the chair at a moment's notice—somewhat analogous to being ready to fight—except that this higher level of alert, of preparedness, meant that they got to see the doctor two seconds sooner. They were as tense as racehorses at the gate. The cardiologists started thinking about it and thought that maybe this was a marker for increased risk of heart disease. Thus began the concept of Type A versus Type B individuals. Type A individuals approached their visit with the doctor—as they did the rest of their lives—more aggressively, and this contributed to their heart disease. Behavior that is good for war is bad for your health in peacetime. Type As always felt more time pressure than Type Bs, the need to get more done, the need to bark at that sales assistant who is slow, the need to honk at the driver ahead who waits a second before going on green. One of the more amazing things is that the doctor who opened our eyes to the Type A concept was originally Type A himself, suffered from angina at age 45 and two heart attacks at 55. But he recognized his problem and learned to modify his own behavior, to the extent that he lived to 90.

Dr. Meyer Friedman, who started life as a Type A who had already decided in junior high school that he should go to Yale undergraduate and Johns Hopkins for medical school, founded an institute that helped Type As learn more Type B behavior. He observed that Type As typically wore a hostile grimace. Remarkably, in some of his behavior modification sessions, he would have his patients concentrate on smiling. He would often tell his patients, "Sweetness is not weakness." When they resisted, he quoted Hamlet: "Assume the virtue even if you have it not... for its use almost can change the stamp of nature." So it appears that the great Shakespeare intuited the facial feedback hypothesis long before the rest of us.

Researchers asked whether they could detect an association between the facial expression of anger or hostility and ischemia (insufficient blood flow) in the heart. They observed heart function in real time, looking for abnormalities in heart muscle contraction (secondary to decreased oxygen or ischemia). At the same time, their subjects with known heart disease were asked structured questions while being videotaped. Afterward they analyzed the facial expressions. People who had more ischemia showed more expressions of anger. In addition, ischemia was seen more commonly when their subjects showed false or non-Duchenne smiles. They suggested that the false smiles might represent attempts at managing or inhibiting the anger.

I would suggest that botulinum toxin should help those whose heart disease is worsened or caused by their Type A behavior, by their hostility, by their anger. Feelings of anger or hostility are causing all sorts of bad hormones to circulate in their blood, stressing their hearts. This is probably a large percentage of those who suffer from heart disease. Which makes me wonder how many Buddhist monks suffer from heart disease? They seem so calm on the outside—are they just as calm on the inside? I don't know the answer, but I suspect that fewer monks suffer from heart disease than those of us who are impatient, overscheduled, and ready to leap from the chair in the waiting room.

OUR EMOTIONAL UNDERSTANDING of the world around us is literally embodied in the same neurons and muscles that allow us to feel, to express ourselves. Our facial muscles help us make sense of our social world by mirroring expressions of those around us, providing our minds with insight into their emotions and thoughts. What does this tell us about other effects of botulinum toxin?

Researchers have found that when it comes to reading expressions of emotion on the faces of people in photographs, women who received botulinum toxin injections around their eyes were less accurate (70 percent vs. 77 percent) than control patients who had their lines injected with a cosmetic filler. Clearly, most of the time, we can still correctly interpret facial expressions without using our facial muscles. We have other neuronal pathways that don't require our facial muscles to interpret the faces of those around us. We are built with multiple wiring mechanisms to get the job done. But we don't do it quite as well when we can't move our faces. Our emotions do not exist in a vacuum— they use our bodies, our muscles, for their full expression. It is possible that by decreasing the activity of certain facial muscles, we may also lessen our ability to feel the pain of others. Perhaps both the intensity and duration of emotions are decreased. For those who suffer from depression, this may be a good thing, as they feel the pain of others only too well, thus reinforcing their own negative thoughts.

If botulinum toxin might inhibit our ability to recognize emotions in others, how does it affect the ability of others to recognize our emotions? One would think that it should be more difficult for others to read us if our faces were less expressive. Most of the reading is unconscious, but it is happening all the time nonetheless. Your ability to bluff in poker may be enhanced. It's interesting to note that many professional card players wear large dark sunglasses in tournaments; I suspect that they have already figured out the importance of facial expression in betraying feelings and thoughts. Perhaps a little botulinum toxin would allow them to play without glasses.

I also wonder how botulinum toxin could affect one's ability to lie convincingly. Since botulinum toxin inhibits the unconscious facial expressions that tell the truth, it could impede the ability to detect liars. We know that facial expressions actually cause changes in our heart rate, sweating, skin conductivity, and other parts of our ANS. The polygraph (lie detector) test is based on monitoring those same parameters. I think it is likely that botulinum toxin could diminish the changes one sees on polygraphs when a person is lying.

One unanswered question is the emotional effect of treating the crow's feet around the eyes. These muscles characterize a "true" or Duchenne smile. Could inhibiting these muscles diminish the enjoyment one feels inside from smiling? Could your ability to feel happiness, regardless of smiling, be reduced? Would the area of the brain that normally lights up when you are happy, the left anterior cortex, be less active? It's hard to make a recommendation without any data, but I raise the possibility that treating the crow's feet alone might not be good for someone who is depressed. It's unusual for anyone to request treatment of only the crow's feet around the eyes—perhaps that is why botulinum toxin patients are generally happier—they usually ask that their frowns be treated at the same time.

How would other kinds of cosmetic surgery affect emotions and moods? Certainly the industry revolves around the concept that if you look better, you will feel better. There is some truth to this. But this kind of mood change may be temporary. How long does one stay happier after winning the lottery? Not very long, according to research. A few months after winning millions, your mood returns to baseline. A facelift may make you look younger, more attractive, and more vigorous, but your mood does not necessarily improve. Facelifts are not a recognized treatment for depression. Removing lines and wrinkles may improve your self-image but should not be assumed to make you happy.

Who should think twice before getting botulinum toxin? It certainly might be more difficult for actors to express the full range of expressions after a treatment. How convincingly could you play Othello if you always looked peaceful? A character actor might want to proceed cautiously before decreasing his or her ability to create facial expressions.

Botulinum toxin might increase the time it takes to get angry—enough so that it might impair your performance in a boxing ring, on the football field, or in any sport where immediate anger might be helpful. We know it slows down your ability to comprehend angry sentences. You might also appear less dangerous, less formidable to an opponent. However, in situations such as directing a complex battlefield, where anger or fear may actually cause you to freeze and impede your ability to make quick and logical decisions, remaining calmer might help win the day.

Would one's ability as a therapist be enhanced or reduced by botulinum toxin? On the one hand, your therapist might be able to remain more detached emotionally after botulinum toxin, allowing her to be more objective. On the other hand, she might be less understanding of your situation. One could make arguments for either conclusion. The answers to these and other questions should prove fascinating as we learn more about the complex and unexpected roles that facial expressions play in our mental health.

NOTES

CHAPTER 1 A POISON TO SOME: A MIRACLE TO OTHERS

XXX **Today, Botox has become:** Facial treatment with botulinum toxin has become the most common cosmetic procedure, with at least several million per year (American Society of Plastic Surgeons Report of the 2010 Plastic Surgery Statistics, http://www.plastic-surgery.org/Documents/news-resources/statistics/2010-statisticss/Top-Level/2010-US-cosmetic-reconstructive-plastic-surgery-minimally-invasive-statistics2.pdf).

XXX **Justinus Kerner:** Erbguth, F. J. (2004, March 19). Historical notes on botulism, *Clostridium botulinum*, botulinum toxin, and the idea of the therapeutic use of the toxin. *Movement Disorders, 19* (Suppl. 8), S2–S6.

XXX **It wasn't until 1973:** Scott, A. B. (1989, September). Botulinum toxin therapy of eye muscle disorders: safety and effectiveness: ophthalmic procedures assessment recommendation. *Ophthalmology* (Suppl.), 37–41.

XXX **Alastair and Jean's seminal research:** Carruthers, J. D., & Carruthers, J. A. (1992, January). Treatment of glabellar frown lines with C. Botulinum-A exotoxin. *The Journal of Dermatologic Surgery and Oncology, 18* (1), 17–21.

XXX   **Botox is now approved:** www.allergan.com/products/medical_dermatology/botox.htm

CHAPTER 2   LESSONS FROM SALPÊTRIÈRE

XXX   **American philosopher and psychologist:** James, W. (1890). *The principles of psychology.* New York: Holt.

XXX   **Long ago Darwin:** Darwin, C. R. (1872). *The expression of emotion in man and animals.* London: Murray. An amazingly prescient and still relevant book.

XXX   **Salpêtrière hospital:** for a review of this hospital and hysteria, Asti Hustvedt's *Medical muses: Hysteria in nineteenth-century Paris* (New York: W. W. Norton, 2011) is a great read and reference. She carefully re-creates the time and context for you.

XXX   **Sigmund Freud was a student:** Breuer, J., & Freud, S. (2004). *Studies on hysteria* (Nicola Lockhurst, Trans.). New York: Basic Books. The classic.

XXX   **Jonathan Cole, an English neurologist:** Cole, J. (1998). *About face.* Cambridge, MA: MIT Press. This book helped get me starting thinking about facial expressions. Thank you, Dr. Cole.

XXX   **Our emotions are critical:** LeDoux, J. (1998). *The emotional brain: The mysterious underpinnings of emotional life.* New York: Touchstone. One of the leaders in the field explains emotions.

XXX   **Here is how one Parkinson's patient:** Peter Dunlap-Shohl writes about his experiences with Parkinson's disease at http://offandonakpdrag.blogspot.com/.

CHAPTER 3   FACIAL EXPRESSIONS

XXX   **Yet psychologists:** Carrere, S., Buehlman, K. T., Gottman, J. M., Coan, J. A., & Ruckstuhl, L. (2000). Predicting marital stability and divorce in newlywed couples. *Journal of Family Psychology, 14* (1).

XXX   **One can trace:** Burrows, A. M. (2008). The facial expression musculature in primates and its evolutionary significance. *BioEssays, 30* (3), 212–225.

XXX   **Darwin's work:** Darwin, C. R. (1872). *The expression of emotion in man and animals.* London: Murray.

XXX   **Without emotion:** Damasio, A. R. (1994). *Descartes' error: Emotion, reason, and the human brain.* New York: HarperCollins. A brilliant book by a great synthesizer.

XXX   **To try and solve:** Ekman, P. (2007). *Emotions revealed: Recognizing faces and feelings to improve communication and emotional life.* New York: Owl Books. The expert in the field. A must read. Read this book several times to pick up on all the nuances.

XXX   **Judo athletes at Olympic:** Matsumoto, D., & Willingham, B. (2009). Spontaneous facial expressions of emotion of blind individuals. *Journal of Personality and Social Psychology, 96* (1), 1–10.

XXX   **Psychologists have been:** Ekman, P. (2006). Cross cultural studies of facial expression. In *Darwin and facial expression* (pp. 169–222). Cambridge, MA: Malor Books.

XXX   **As Darwin wrote:** Darwin, C. R. (1872). *The expression of emotion in man and animals.* London: Murray.

XXX   **very brief micro-expressions:** Ekman, P. (2007). *Emotions revealed: Recognizing faces and feelings to improve communication and emotional life* (p. 214). New York: Owl Books.

CHAPTER 4   THE MUSCLE OF JOY

XXX   **We have seen so many:** Trumble, A. (2004). *A brief history of the smile.* New York: Basic Books.

XXX **Auguste Dupin:** Poe, Edgar Allan. (1844). *The purloined letter.* Ekman references this in his book, *Emotions revealed: Recognizing faces and feelings to improve communication and emotional life.* New York: Owl Books.

XXX **The scientific analysis of the smile:** Duchenne de Boulogne, G.-B. (1990). *The mechanism of human facial expression* (A. Cuthbertson, Ed. and Trans.). New York: Cambridge University Press. (Original publication 1862)

XXX **How important is a smile:** Shaw, W. C., Rees, G., Dawe, M., & Charles, C. R. (1985). The influence of dentofacial appearance on the social attractiveness of young adults. *American Journal of Orthodontics, 87,* 21–26.

XXX **complexities of smiling:** Provine, R. R. (2000). *Laughter: A scientific investigation.* New York: Penguin. A great resource on laughter and smiling.

XXX **One study:** Langlois, J. H., Kalakanis, L., Rubenstein, A. J., Larson, A., Hallam, M., & Smoot, M. (2000). Maxims or myths of beauty? A meta-analytic and theoretical review. *Psychological Bulletin, 126,* 390–423.

XXX **Those baseball players:** Abel, E. L., & Kruger, M. L. (2010, April). Smile intensity in photographs predicts longevity. *Psychological Science, 21,* 542–544

XXX **To probe for cause:** VanSwearingen, J. M., Cohn, J. F., Turnbull, J., Mrzai, T., & Johnson, P. (1998, June). Psychological distress: linking impairment with disability in facial neuromotor disorders. *Otolaryngology—Head and Neck Surgery, 118* (6), 790–796.

XXX **This monk's left prefrontal:** Lutz, A., Greischar, L. L., Rawlings, N. B., Ricard, M., & Davidson, R. J. (2004). Long-term meditators self-induce high-amplitude gamma synchrony during mental practice. *PNAS, 101* (46), 16369–16373.

XXX   **Can eight weeks:** Hall, S. S. (2003, September 14). Is Buddhism good for your health? *New York Times Magazine.* Follow the trail of brilliant research of Davidson on mediation.

CHAPTER 5   WRINKLER ABOVE
THE EYE

XXX   **The corrugator:** Ekman, P. (2007). *Emotions revealed: Recognizing faces and feelings to improve communication and emotional life.* New York: Owl Books.

CHAPTER 6   COMMUNICATION FROM THE
UNCONSCIOUS: A WINDOW INTO FEELINGS

XXX   **In monkeys the amygdala:** Angleton, J. P., & Passingham, R. E. (1981). Syndrome produced by lesions of the amygdala in monkeys (Macaca mulatta). *Journal of Comparative and Physiological Psychology, 95* (6), 961–977.

XXX   **When you hear:** LeDoux, J. (1998). *The emotional brain: the mysterious underpinnings of emotional life.* New York: Touchstone.

XXX   **Sometimes difficulties:** Klein, Jeffrey A. (2000). *Tumescent technique: tumescent anesthesia & microcannular liposuction.* St. Louis: Mosby.

XXX   **As Oliver Sacks:** Oliver Sacks. (1985). *The man who mistook his wife for a hat and other clinical tales.* New York: Simon and Schuster.

CHAPTER 7   DARWIN AND
FACIAL FEEDBACK

XXX   **There is actually:** Adelmann, P. K., & Zajonc, R. B. (1989). Facial efference and the experience of emotion. *Annual Review of Psychology, 40,* 249–280. An influential review.

XXX   **Andrew Elmore:** Springen, K. (2006, May). Can you really Botox the blues away? *Newsweek*.

XXX   **The great German:** Gotthold Lessing, quoted in Fidlund, A. J. (1991). Evolution and facial action in reflex, social motive and paralanguage. *Biological Psychology, 32*, 3–100. Mentioned by Cole in About Face.

XXX   **In the first half:** Bell, C. (1824). *Essays on the anatomy and philosophy of expression.* London: John Murray.

XXX   **Darwin picked up:** Darwin, C. R. (1872). *The expression of emotion in man and animals.* London: Murray.

XXX   **He stressed the concept:** Tomkins, S. (1962). *Affect, imagery, consciousness.* New York: Springer.

XXX   **I began the project:** Ekman, P. (2007). *Emotions revealed: recognizing faces and feelings to improve communication and emotional life* (p. 2). New York: Owl Books.

XXX   **Eric Kandel:** Kandel, E. (2012). *The age of insight: the quest to understand the unconscious in art, mind and brain; from Vienna 1900 to the present.* New York: Random House. An amazing synthesis of art and neuroscience.

XXX   **To try and eliminate:** Strack, R., Martin, L. L., & Stepper, S. (1988). Inhibiting and facilitating conditions of facial expressions: a nonobtrusive test of the facial feedback hypothesis. *Journal of Personality and Social Psychology, 54*, 768–777.

XXX   **To test the facial feedback:** Larsen, R. J., Kasimatis, M., & Frey, K. (1992). Facilitating the furrowed brow: an unobtrusive test of the facial feedback hypothesis applied to unpleasant affect. *Cognition and Emotion, 6*, 321–338.

XXX   **contained the vowel *u*:** Zajonc, R. B., Murphy, S. T., & Inglehart, M. (1989). Feeling and facial efference: implications of the vascular theory of emotion. *Psychological Review, 96* (3), 394–416.

XXX   **Now let us take a real-world:** Strack, F., & Neumann, R. (2000). Furrowing the brow may undermine perceived fame: the role of facial feedback in judgments of celebrity. *Personality and Social Psychology Bulletin, 26,* 762–768.

XXX   **Fear is one well-studied:** LeDoux, J. (1998). *The emotional brain: The mysterious underpinnings of emotional life.* New York: Touchstone. A very readable explanation of emotions by an original researcher in the field.

XXX   **I put my face:** Charles Darwin, quoted in Ekman, P. (2007). *Emotions revealed: recognizing faces and feelings to improve communication and emotional life.* New York: Owl Books.

XXX   **riding up the elevator:** Williams, L. E., & Bargh, J. A. (2008). Experiencing physical warmth promotes interpersonal warmth. *Science, 322* (5901), 606–607.

XXX   **achievement test:** Stepper, S., & Strack, F. (1993). Proprioceptive determinants of emotional and nonemotional feelings. *Journal of Personality and Social Psychology, 64* (2), 211–220.

XXX   **Antonio Damasio:** Damasio, A. R. (1994). *Descartes' error: Emotion, reason, and the human brain.* New York: HarperCollins.

XXX   **Researchers decided:** Ekman, P., Levenson, R. W., & Friesen, W. V. (1983). Autonomic nervous system activity distinguishes among emotions. *Science, 221* (4616), 1208–1210.

XXX   **amygdala is a key player:** Fusar-Poli, P., Placentino, A., Carletti, F., Landi, P., Allen, P., Surguladze, S., et al. (2009). Functional atlas of emotional faces processing: a voxel-based meta-analysis of 105 functional magnetic resonance imaging studies. *Journal of Psychiatry and Neuroscience, 34* (6), 418–432.

XXX   **Another theory:** Adelmann, P. K., & Zajonc, R. B. (1989). Facial efference and the experience of emotion. *Annual Review of Psychology, 40,* 249–280.

XXX   **Researchers asked:** Hennenlotter, A., Dresel, C., Castrop, F., Ceballo-Baumann, A. O., Wohlschläger, A. M., & Haslinger, B. (2009, March). The link between facial feedback and neural activity within central circuitries of emotion—new insights from botulinum toxin-induced denervation of frown muscles. *Cerebral Cortex, 19* (3), 537–542.

CHAPTER 8   EMBODIED EMOTION

XXX   **Here is Darwin's:** Darwin, C. R. (1872). *The expression of emotion in man and animals.* London: Murray.

XXX   **I once watched:** Darwin, C. R. (1872). *The expression of emotion in man and animals.* London: Murray.

XXX   **"Omega Melancholium":** Greden, J. F., Genero, N., & Price, H. L. (1985). Agitation-increased electromyogram activity in the corrugator muscle region: a possible explanation of the "Omega sign"? *American Journal of Psychiatry, 142,* 348–351.

XXX   **To answer this question:** Schwartz, G. E., Fair, P. L., Salt, P., Mandel, M. R., & Klerman, G. L. (1976). Facial muscle patterning to affective imagery in depressed and nondepressed subjects. *Science, 192,* 489–491.

XXX   **It may be that what:** Teasdale, J. D., & Bancroft, J. (1977). Manipulation of thought content as a determinant of mood and corrugator electromyographic activity in depressed patients. *Journal of Abnormal Psychology, 86* (3), 235–241.

XXX   **In another study:** Sirota, A. D., Schwartz, G. E., & Kristeller, J. L. (1987). Facial muscle activity during induced mood states: differential growth and carry-over of elated versus depressed patterns. *Psychophysiology, 24* (6), 691–699.

XXX   **Even reading a single word:** Niedenthal, P. M., Winkielman, P., Mondillon, L., & Vermeulen, N. (2009). Embodiment of emotion concepts. *Journal of Personality and Social Psychology, 96* (6), 1120–1136.

XXX   **I have treated:** Finzi, E., & Wasserman, E. (2006). Treatment of depression with botulinum toxin A: a case series. *Journal of Dermatologic Surgery, 32,* 645–650.

XXX   **Researchers compared the mood:** Lewis, M. B., & Bowler, P. J. (2009). Botulinum toxin cosmetic therapy correlates with a more positive mood. *Journal of Cosmetic Dermatology, 8,* 24–26.

XXX   **Another group of researchers:** Dayan, S. H., Arkins, J. P., Patel, A. B., & Gal, T. J. (2010, December). A double-blind, randomized, placebo-controlled health-outcomes survey of the effect of botulinum toxin type a injections on quality of life and self-esteem. *Dermatologic Surgery, 36* (Suppl. 4), 2088–2097.

XXX   **The gold standard:** Wollmer, M. A., de Boer, C., Kalak, N., Beck, J., Götz, T., Schmidt, T., et al. (2012, May). Facing depression with botulinum toxin: a randomized controlled trial. *Journal of Psychiatric Research, 46* (5), 574–581.

XXX   **First, what happens:** Ruhé, H. G., Booij, J., Veltman, D. J., Michel, M. C., & Schene, A. H. (2012, April). Successful pharmacologic treatment of major depressive disorder attenuates amygdala activation to negative facial expressions: a functional magnetic resonance imaging study. *Journal of Clinical Psychiatry, 73* (4), 451–459.

XXX   **Does Botox:** Hennenlotter, A., Dresel, C., Castrop, F., Ceballo-Baumann, A. O., Wohlschläger, A. M., & Haslinger, B. (2009, March). The link between facial feedback and neural activity within central circuitries of emotion—new insights from botulinum toxin-induced denervation of frown muscles. *Cerebral Cortex, 19* (3), 537–542.

CHAPTER 9   LAUGHTER

XXX   **Joy, when intense:** Darwin, C. R. (1872). *The expression of emotion in man and animals.* London: Murray.

XXX   **Laughter looks so:** Provine, R. R. (2000). *Laughter: a scientific investigation.* New York: Penguin. We are fortunate that Dr. Provine dedicated himself to laughter.

XXX   **In southern India:** Provine, R. R. (2000). *Laughter: a scientific investigation* (p. 30). New York: Penguin.

XXX   **Human laughter:** Gervais, M., & Wilson, D. S. (2005, December). The evolution and functions of laughter and humor: A synthetic approach. *Quarterly Review of Biology, 80* (4), 395–430.

XXX   **It was a summer day:** Blakeslee, S. (2006, January 10). Cells that read minds. *New York Times.*

XXX   **Years later:** Cousins N. (1976). Anatomy of an illness (as perceived by the patient). *New England Journal of Medicine, 295*, 1458–1463.

XXX   **Can laughing actually:** Matsuzaki, T., Nakajima, A., Ishigami, S., Tanno, M., & Yoshino, S. (2006, February.) Mirthful laughter differentially affects serum pro- and anti-inflammatory cytokine levels depending on the level of disease activity in patients with rheumatoid arthritis. *Rheumatology, 45* (2), 182–186.

XXX   **How could laughter:** Miller, M., & Fry, W. F. (2009, November).The effect of mirthful laughter on the human cardiovascular system. *Medical Hypotheses, 73* (5), 636–639.

XXX   **funny one-hour video:** Bennett, M. P., Zeller, J. M., Rosenberg, L., & McCann, J. (2003, March–April). The effect of mirthful laughter on stress and natural killer cell activity. *Alternative Therapies in Health and Medicine, 9* (2), 38–45.

XXX   **important antibody:** Bennett, M. P., & Lengacher, C. (2009). Humor and laughter may influence health IV. Humor and immune function. *Evidence-Based Complementary and Alternative Medicine, 6* (2), 159–164.

CHAPTER 10   PESSIMISM, DEPRESSION, AND OPTIMISM

XXX   **In the cognitive model:** Seligman, M. E. P. (1975). *Helplessness: on depression, development, and death.* San Francisco: W. H. Freeman.

XXX   **Can you:** Peterson, C., Seligman, M. E., & Vaillant, G. E. (1988, July). Pessimistic explanatory style is a risk factor for physical illness: a thirty-five-year longitudinal study. *Journal of Personality and Social Psychology, 55* (1), 23–27.

XXX   **"broken heart syndrome":** Wittstein, I. S., Thiemann, D. R., Lima, J. A. C., Baughman, K. L., Schulman, S. P., Gerstenblith, G., et al. (2005). Neurohumoral features of myocardial stunning due to sudden emotional stress. *New England Journal of Medicine, 352,* 539–548.

XXX   **Dr. Roy Ziegelstein:** Flynn, R. (2008, Summer). Troubled minds, troubled hearts. *Hopkins Medicine.*

XXX   **your immune system:** Dunn, G. P., Bruce, A. T., Ikeda, H., Old, L. J., & Schreiber, R. D. (2002). Cancer immunoediting: from immunosurveillance to tumor escape. *Nature Immunology, 3* (11), 991–998.

CHAPTER 11   NON-COSMETIC COSMETIC SURGERY

XXX   **definitely contagious:** Hatfield, E., Cacioppo, J. T., & Rapson, R. L. (1993). Emotional contagion. *Current Directions in Psychological Sciences, 2,* 96–99.

CHAPTER 12   FUTURE DIRECTIONS

XXX   **Fred Mohs figured out:** Mohs, F. E., & Mikhail, G. R. (1991). *Mohs micrographic surgery.* Philadelphia: W. B. Saunders

XXX   **Sixty-five:** Friedman, M., & Rosenman, R. H. (1974). *Type A behavior and your heart.* New York: Knopf.

XXX   **hostility and ischemia:** Rosenberg, E. L., Ekman, P., Jiang, W., Babyak, M., Coleman, R. E., Hanson, M., et al. (2001, June). Linkages between facial expressions of anger and transient myocardial ischemia in men with coronary artery disease. *Emotion, 1* (2), 107–115.

XXX   **faces of people:** Neal, D. T., & Chartrand, T. L. (2011). Embodied emotion perception: amplifying and dampening facial feedback modulates emotion perception accuracy. *Social Psychological and Personality Science, 2* (6), 673–678.

CPSIA information can be obtained at www.ICGtesting.com
Printed in the USA
BVOW081928181012

303340BV00002B/2/P